INSTANTLY
FRENCH!

INSTANTLY FRENCH!

Classic French Recipes for Your

Electric Pressure Cooker

ANN MAH

St. Martin's Griffin

New York

www.stmartins.com

Designed by Michelle McMillian

Inside cover illustration copyright © Franzi/Shutterstock.com
Shutterstock images pages 67, 86, 172, 183

The Library of Congress Cataloging-in-Publication Data is available upon request.

ISBN 978-1-250-18444-3 (trade paperback)
ISBN 978-1-250-18445-0 (ebook)

Our books may be purchased in bulk for promotional, educational, or business use. Please contact
your local bookseller or the Macmillan Corporate and Premium Sales Department at 1-800-221-7945,
extension 5442, or by email at MacmillanSpecialMarkets@macmillan.com.

First Edition: September 2018

10 9 8 7 6 5 4 3 2 1

For my parents,
who introduced me to the world of
pressure cooking

Contents

1. FIRST COURSES / *LES ENTRÉES*

2. SOUPS / *LES SOUPES*

3. CHICKEN / *LE POULET*

6. VEGETABLES / LES LEGUMES

7. DESSERTS / LES DESSERTS

Acknowledgments

My thanks to Michael Flamini, Gwen Hawkes, and all the team at St Martin's Press, including Jordan Hanley, Justine Sha, Michelle McMillian, Eric C. Meyer, and Kerri Resnick. Heartfelt thanks to Deborah Schneider, Penelope Burns, Cathy Gleason, and the team at Gelfman Schneider/ICM Partners for their unflagging support.

Thanks to Ashley McLaughlin, who is a pleasure to work with. She perfectly captured the spirit of this book with her beautiful photographs.

Thanks to Jérôme Avenas, Shamroon Aziz, Kristen Beddard, Soisick Gaonac'h, Christian Conley Holthausen, Allie Larkin, Michael King, Erin Reeser, Thomas Regan-Lefebvre, Steve Rhinds, and Lucy Vanel, who offered cooking advice, suggestions, and ideas.

Thanks also to Karen Kornbluh, Fernando Laguardo, and Anne Schwartz, who provided valuable feedback.

Special thanks to David Lebovitz for his generous encouragement—and for allowing me to adapt his chocolate cake recipe.

My love and thanks to Christopher Klein and Lutetia Klein, who make meals a joy.

Introduction

One of the first things I noticed when I moved to Paris ten years ago is that time moves more slowly in France. Shopping in the open market, ordering coffee at the café, or even dropping off clothes at the dry cleaner are all tasks that proceed at a stately pace. This sense of leisure extends to the kitchen, where *les cocottes de Mémé*—Granny's slow-simmered dishes, like cassoulet, boeuf bourguignon, or *blanquette de veau*—form some of the earliest childhood memories. Above all, French people adore small indulgences—and time is, perhaps, the great luxury of all.

As an ardent Francophile and enthusiastic home cook, I have long loved preparing French meals, elegant affairs that unfurl over four courses of *entrée* (appetizer), *plat* (main course), *fromage* (cheese), and *dessert* (a universal word of joy). But when my husband and I welcomed a baby daughter, my time and patience for lengthy meals grew short. Cooking became a form of survival, and eating solely about sustenance. I would look at my beloved cast-iron Dutch oven and give a wistful sigh for all the hearty French braises, soups, and stews of yore.

And then my dad sent me a multifunction pressure cooker. I admit, I was skeptical at first. Too many viewings of the exploding dinner scene in *Breakfast at Tiffany's* had made me wary of pressure cookers. Also, like anyone who lives in an urban—i.e., cramped—environment, I am averse to single-use gadgets. And yet my friends raved about them, swapping recipes and tips with an almost cult-like devotion.

One Saturday morning, I finally gave the thing a shot, pressure-cooking a pot of beans with the tentative push of a button. Thirty minutes later, I had a batch of astonishingly delicious, uniformly creamy beans—they were, in fact, the best beans I had ever cooked. I began experimenting with other recipes, my delight and amazement growing with each dish.

Hard cubes of winter squash softened in ten minutes. Tough cuts of meat became fork-tender in less than half an hour. And in almost all cases, the pressure cooker made food that was more delicious—more tender, more velvety, more luxurious—than I could produce from hours of simmering.

When I began talking to French friends about this newfangled device, I was surprised to find that their passion for the pressure cooker matched my own. As I discovered, French households have relied on the conventional pressure cooker for decades. In fact, they seem to regard it with a nostalgia more powerful than Proust's emotions for the madeleine. "I grew up with the constant whistling of the pressure cooker, and I find the music of it pretty soothing," said my friend Thomas.

Called *la cocotte-minute*, the pressure cooker was invented by a French physicist, Denis Papin, in the seventeenth century—and it has long been considered a secret weapon among French home cooks. "As a busy parent, my *maman* would use her pressure cooker every day," my friend Jérôme told me. Indeed, with its ability to speedily render tough cuts of meat spoon-tender, the pressure cooker is ideal for the hearty braises that are the hallmark of great French cuisine. Savvy French cooks also use it as a kitchen shortcut, to quickly soften winter squash for a gratin, for example, or endives for *endives au jam-bon*. In many French home kitchens, the pressure cooker is always at hand—even at the expense of precious real estate—because it's such a useful tool. Rather than keep the device in the back of a cupboard, it's stored on a convenient shelf so it's always ready for use.

The beauty of the multifunction cooker, however, is that it's more than a pressure cooker—it also offers options to sauté, steam, slow cook, and even make rice or yogurt. Aside from meaty mains, the device can help prepare vegetarian dishes, elegant starters, soups, and desserts—with ease and speed. In this book, the chapters are organized by courses, but all the recipes (except desserts) are designed to work as stand-alone dishes, satisfying enough for a meal, paired with cheese, bread, or a simple salad on the side.

These days, I divide my time between Paris and Washington, DC, and my appetite for French cuisine—with its appreciation for home-cooked, seasonal food—remains undiminished. And though I—like most working people—still struggle to find the time and energy to cook every day, the multifunction pressure cooker has allowed me to reclaim all the recipes that felt too laborious to tackle. In this book, I share these recipes, along with tips from French pressure cooker aficionados, shortcuts, observations on French culture, and advice for using

the multifunction pressure cooker to create authentic French food. Finally, elegant French fare is accessible every day!

ABOUT YOUR MULTIFUNCTION PRESSURE COOKER

For a generation of French people, there is a similar childhood memory of "the stain"—imprinted on the kitchen ceiling, an indelible reminder of that time Maman's pressure cooker terrifyingly exploded. Happily, today's modern technology means electric pressure cookers have built-in safety functions that ensure explosions never happen. There is absolutely no need to be afraid!

There are a few popular brands of multifunction pressure cookers, such as Breville Fast Slow Pro, Fagor 3-in-1, and Instant Pot. They all operate similarly, but each one has its own system. It is essential that you read the instruction manual that comes with your device. I tested these recipes in a 6-quart Instant Pot, and that's the size I recommend for everyday cooking. But for the recipes here, the larger 8-quart size also works.

In this book, I refer to various functions and parts of the multifunction pressure cooker:

Pressure cooking: There are two settings, low pressure and high pressure. The recipes in this book specify which one to use, though the default is generally high pressure. *Note:* When you start a new recipe, make sure the machine's setting is appropriate for what you are about to cook. Otherwise, the results could be an unpleasant surprise.

Sauté function: Used without the lid to sauté vegetables, to brown or sear meat before braising, or to simmer and reduce liquids after cooking.

Yogurt function: There are two settings to make yogurt. The first, "Boil," scalds and pasteurizes the milk, while the second, "Yogurt," gently heats the inoculated milk for eight hours, allowing for fermentation.

Manual release of steam: This is the fastest way to release the pressure from your cooker. Using a long-handled wooden spoon (or similar), carefully flip the steam-release valve so hot steam gushes from the cooker. Note that the steam is intense and blistering hot, so it's important to avoid contact with your face and hands. Also note that the steam can coat kitchen surfaces with an unpleasant film.

Natural pressure release: This is the gentler and slower method to release steam from the pressure cooker. When the pressure cooker has finished cooking, wait for its contents to naturally cool enough for the float valve to drop. Depending on the amount of food in the pressure cooker, this can take anywhere from 15 to 45 minutes. A damp towel placed on the lid can hasten the process.

Inner pot: This is the removable stainless-steel pot in which all the food cooks. It cleans easily, but any persistent stains can be scrubbed away with distilled white vinegar.

Steam valve: This is a loose and jiggly handle located on top of the pressure cooker's lid. The valve needs to be locked to allow pressure to build. Flip it in the opposite direction to unlock the valve and release the built-up steam and pressure.

Float valve: Also located in the lid, this red button pops up when the pressure cooker's contents are under pressure and drops once all the steam has released.

Zero (0) minute pressure cooking time: Using the buttons on the cooker, you can adjust the cooking time to zero (0). This means that the cooker comes to pressure before you immediately release the steam. This technique is good for delicate, quick-cooking foods like fish, or vegetables that benefit from precooking, such as the cauliflower in *gratin au chou-fleur*.

SPECIAL EQUIPMENT

I am not a fan of single-use kitchen gadgets. But there are a few tools that are useful when cooking with these devices.

Trivet or steaming rack: This small metal stand is included with most multifunction pressure cookers. It's useful for steaming vegetables or fish, as well as custards or other food cooked in ramekins or dishes.

8-inch round dish: Some foods, like delicate fish fillets or whole apples, benefit from being cooked in a dish. Make sure your vessel lacks handles so that it will fit in the inner pot. I recommend an 8-inch round soufflé dish.

7- or 8-inch springform pan: The standard springform pan is 10 inches, which is too large to fit in the inner pot. To make cakes and other sweets in the multifunction pressure cooker, look for a smaller 7- or 8-inch pan in your local cookware shop, or order one online.

Instant-read thermometer: Essential for taking a quick, accurate temperature in order to make yogurt or test the doneness of country pâté.

Mason jars: These jars are useful for the book's country pâté recipe (page 7). You can also use them to prepare individual jars of yogurt directly in the multicooker. For maximum flexibility, I recommend choosing a short, wide jar with clean lines. The French brand Le Parfait is popular and can be found in cookware shops or ordered online.

High altitude tips

Because the temperature of boiling water increases above sea level, elevation can greatly affect the pressure cooker, increasing the amount of cooking time. The general rule of thumb is that you should increase the pressure-cooking time by 5 percent for every 1,000 feet after 2,000 feet above sea level. But I suggest checking the internet for an exact calculation.

1

FIRST COURSES
Les Entrées

Poached Leeks, Walnut Oil Vinaigrette, and Walnuts

Poireaux vinaigrette

Serves 4

Leeks are a quintessential French vegetable, and they appear everywhere in French cuisine, from soups to stews. Economical and healthy, poireaux vinaigrette is a classic bistro starter, a simple salad of poached leeks drizzled with tangy vinaigrette dressing. Here chopped walnuts give a delicate crunch, their warm flavor echoed by the walnut oil in the vinaigrette. For a light lunch, accompany with hard-boiled eggs and bread.

1 tablespoon minced shallot

2 tablespoons fresh lemon juice

¼ teaspoon fine salt, plus more as desired

5 leeks

¼ cup (30 grams) chopped walnuts

1 teaspoon Dijon mustard

3 tablespoons walnut oil

3 tablespoons mild-tasting olive oil

Freshly ground black pepper

1. Combine the shallot, lemon juice, and salt in a small bowl, and leave to marinate for at least 5 minutes to take the bite out of the shallot.

2. Prepare the leeks by slicing the root end off very close to the root so that the individual interior leaves do not separate. Cut each leek in half lengthwise and remove the tough, fibrous exterior leaves. Rinse each leek thoroughly to remove all the grit from between the leaves.

3. Place the steaming rack in the pressure cooker and add 1 cup (250 ml) water. Arrange the leeks on top of the rack. Cook on high pressure for 1 minute.

4. While the leeks are cooking, in a skillet, toast the walnuts over medium heat until golden, about 3 minutes. Remove from the heat and allow to cool.

5. Finish preparing the vinaigrette by whisking the mustard into the lemon juice and shallots. While whisking, slowly drizzle in the walnut and olive oils until fully incorporated. Season with pepper, taste, and adjust the seasonings. Chop the cooled toasted walnuts.

6. When the leeks have finished cooking, manually release the steam. Remove the leeks and arrange as shown. Drizzle the leeks generously with the vinaigrette and sprinkle the walnuts all over the top. Serve warm or at room temperature.

Chickpeas and Grated Carrots with Cumin and Lemon Zest

Salade de pois chiches et carottes

Serves 4–6

One of my favorite places to have lunch in Paris was a little tearoom owned by four women from Tunisia. They served a delicious plat du jour—an assortment of spiced vegetarian stews and salads that changed daily. I always looked forward to the carrot salad, which was spiked with cumin, coriander, and lemon zest. Alas, one day I walked by the restaurant—and it had disappeared! (I later found out they had lost their lease—victims of rising rents.) I missed them so much, I created this chickpea and carrot salad, filled with the flavors of North Africa, as an homage.

FOR THE CHICKPEAS

1 cup (200 grams) dried chickpeas, rinsed and sorted for debris

1 teaspoon fine salt

FOR THE SALAD

½ to 1 small garlic clove, minced

Zest and juice of 1 lemon

1 teaspoon ground cumin

1 teaspoon ground coriander

½ teaspoon fine salt, plus more as desired

1. Prepare the chickpeas: Place the chickpeas in a large bowl, cover with water by 2 inches, and soak for at least 8 hours or up to overnight. Drain the chickpeas and put them in the pressure cooker, along with 4 cups (1 L) water and the salt. Stir to combine. Cook on high pressure for 10 minutes. Allow the pressure to release naturally for 10 minutes, then manually release the remaining steam. (Alternatively, if you don't have time to soak them, put the dried chickpeas, 4 cups (1 L) water, and the salt in the pressure cooker and cook on high pressure for 1 hour. Allow the pressure to release naturally for 10 minutes, then manually release the remaining steam.)

2. While the chickpeas are cooking, prepare the salad: In a large bowl, combine the garlic, lemon zest, lemon juice, cumin, coriander, salt, and pepper. Add the olive oil, whisking until the dressing is combined. Taste and adjust the seasonings.

3. Grate the carrots on the large holes of a box grater. Add the grated carrot to the bowl with the dressing and stir to combine.

(continued)

¼ teaspoon freshly ground
black pepper, plus more
as desired

3 tablespoons extra-virgin
olive oil

2 carrots

¼ cup (15 grams) fresh
cilantro leaves, coarsely
chopped

4. Drain the cooked chickpeas, reserving their cooking liquid, if desired (see Note). Add the warm chickpeas to the bowl with the carrots and dressing. Stir to combine. Toss with the cilantro. Taste and adjust the seasonings, adding more salt and pepper, if desired.

Note: The leftover chickpea cooking liquid has a rich, full-bodied texture and is excellent in soups like Ribs, Stems, Roots, Leaves (page 29).

BEANS: TO SOAK OR NOT TO SOAK?

One of the advantages of the electric pressure cooker is that you can cook dried beans without presoaking them. Thin-skinned legumes like black beans or kidney work particularly well, softening in about 30 minutes, while tougher beans like chickpeas take up to an hour. And yet, even though fast-cooked beans are one of the most magical capabilities of the electric pressure cooker, I still presoak beans if I remember and have time. I find soaked beans turn out creamier, more tender, unsplit, and evenly cooked. Honestly, my advice is to always presoak—it takes less than a minute to throw dried beans in a bowl and cover them with cold water, before leaving them to sit for a few hours. But if you've forgotten—or have a spur-of-the-moment urge for a pot of beans—the pressure cooker can definitely come to the rescue.

Country Pâté

Pâté de campagne

Makes 4 (7- **to 8-ounce / 2**00- to 225-gram) jars

Pâté de campagne is one of the great hallmarks of French cuisine, and it does sound fairly intimidating. But honestly, what is country pâté but a deliciously rich, liver-enhanced meat loaf? Traditionally the mixture of highly seasoned pork and liver is pressed into a terrine, and cooked in a bain-marie (water bath) for over an hour. But dividing the mixture into mason jars and cooking them in the pressure cooker shaves off a considerable amount of time. Pâté de campagne en bocaux—pâté in jars—is popular in France, enjoyed at picnics or wine bars. Though this pâté is not sterilized—and therefore not meant for long-term storage—it is perfect for a convivial evening with friends, and will keep for up to 10 days in the fridge.

---

1 tablespoon (15 grams) unsalted butter

3 shallots (4 ounces / 110 grams), minced

½ pound (250 grams) chicken livers

2 garlic cloves, minced

1 pound (500 grams) ground pork shoulder (see Note)

½ pound (250 grams) ground pork belly

½ teaspoon dried thyme

¼ teaspoon ground allspice

1 tablespoon fine salt

½ teaspoon freshly ground black pepper

1. In a small skillet, melt the butter over medium heat. Add the shallots and cook until softened, 3 to 4 minutes. Remove from the heat.

2. Place the chicken livers in a food processor and pulse briefly, five to seven times, until coarsely ground.

3. In a large bowl, combine the shallots, garlic, chicken livers, pork shoulder, pork belly, thyme, allspice, salt, pepper, egg, and brandy. Stir to combine thoroughly.

4. Pack the pâté mixture into the four jars, filling them to the brim if necessary. Spread a kitchen towel on the counter and firmly tap the bottom of each jar against the counter to tamp down the mixture and eliminate any air pockets. Cover the jars snugly with aluminum foil.

5. Place the steaming rack in the pressure cooker and add 1½ cups (375 ml) water. Arrange the covered jars on the rack. Cook on low pressure for 15 minutes. Allow the pressure to release naturally for 10 minutes, then manually release the remaining pressure.

(continued)

1 large egg

⅓ cup (80 ml) brandy

SPECIAL EQUIPMENT

4 (7- to 8-ounce/ 200- to 225-gram) short mason jars (see Note)

Instant-read thermometer

6. Remove the jars from the pressure cooker and unwrap them. An instant-read thermometer inserted into the center of each pâté should register at least 160°F (70°C). Leave the jars to cool to room temperature.

7. Seal the jars with their lids. Refrigerate for at least 8 hours to solidify and season the pâté before serving. Serve it directly from the jars, accompanied by sliced baguette and cornichons. Store in the refrigerator for up to 10 days.

Notes: The pork needs to be passed through a meat grinder to achieve the proper chunky consistency. If you don't have a meat grinder, ask your butcher to grind the pork shoulder and pork belly for you.

Choose a short, wide mason jar with clean lines so you can slide the pâté from the vessel, if desired. The French brand Le Parfait is popular—it can be found in cookware shops or ordered online.

Artichokes with Creamy Tarragon Vinaigrette

Artichauts vinaigrette à l'estragon

Serves 4–6

Many French families still serve lunch or dinner in four courses—entrée, plat, fromage, dessert—and the first course is often vegetables, because "they fill you up before the main dish," says my friend Thomas. In his family, the steamed artichoke, prepared in the pressure cooker and accompanied by tarragon vinaigrette, has always been the typical summer starter. (As I've discovered, artichokes and tarragon are considered a classic pairing in France, like tomatoes and basil in Italy.) If you can't find tarragon-flavored vinegar, use regular and stir in a pinch of fresh tarragon. Note that the cooking time of the artichokes will vary depending on their size.

4 to 6 globe artichokes (1 per person)

½ lemon (optional)

2 tablespoons white wine tarragon vinegar

1 teaspoon Dijon mustard

Fine salt and freshly ground black pepper

5 tablespoons extra-virgin olive oil

1 to 4 tablespoons sour cream or crème fraîche (as desired)

1 tablespoon minced fresh herbs such as tarragon, parsley, chives, and/or basil (optional)

1. Prepare the artichokes by trimming the stem so the artichokes can stand upright. Using a serrated knife, slice off the top third of each artichoke. Remove any tough outer leaves. Using kitchen shears, cut the sharp thorns from the remaining exterior leaves. Pull out the leaves slightly to loosen them. If desired, rub the lemon against the cut surfaces of each artichoke to prevent browning.

2. Place the steaming rack in the pressure cooker and add 1 cup (250 ml) water. Arrange the artichokes stem-side down on the steaming rack. (Depending on their size, you may have to cook them in batches.) The pressure cooking time will vary depending on the size of the artichokes. Cook on high pressure for 4 to 6 minutes for small artichokes, 8 to 10 minutes for medium, and 12 to 14 for large.

3. While the artichokes cook, prepare the vinaigrette. In a medium bowl, whisk together the vinegar, mustard, ¼ teaspoon salt, and pepper to taste. Slowly whisk the olive oil into the mustard-vinegar mixture. While whisking, add the sour cream 1 tablespoon at a time and whisk to emulsify the sauce. The sour cream will thicken the sauce, so add enough to suit your preference. Stir in the fresh herbs (if using). Taste and season with salt and pepper as desired.

(continued)

4. When the artichokes have finished cooking, manually release the steam. Transfer the artichokes to a plate or cutting board and test them by pulling at a leaf—if it slides out easily, it's done. If there's resistance, return the artichokes to the pressure cooker, close and lock the lid, and allow them to sit in the residual heat for 5 minutes before testing them again.

5. Serve the artichokes warm or at room temperature, dipping the leaves into the tarragon vinaigrette. When you get to the "choke"—the fuzzy center, which in French is called *foin*, or "hay"—use a spoon to scrape it away. Eat the remaining base and stem, which is the artichoke's heart.

WHAT KIND OF CREAM?

Cream is used liberally in the French kitchen, swirled into soups and sauces, or dolloped on desserts like apple tart or stewed fruit. But when I moved to Paris, I was surprised to learn that when French home cooks say *crème*, they almost always mean crème fraîche.

Crème Fraîche

A thick, tangy, fermented cream, crème fraîche is heavy and smooth, and its generous 30% fat content means it doesn't curdle in boiling liquid, making it ideal for thickening sauces. In the States, crème fraîche can be expensive and difficult to find, and I almost always substitute sour cream. Especially when used in strongly flavored sauces, the two are virtually interchangeable.

Sour Cream

Also fermented, sour cream has a rich, luscious texture. But with a lower fat content of 20%, it can curdle when simmered. To sidestep this problem, I usually whisk in sour cream with the pot off the heat.

Heavy Cream

In French, *crème fleurette*, or *crème liquide*, is most commonly used in custards, mousses, or for whipped cream. The latter, called *crème Chantilly*, was reportedly invented at the Château de Chantilly outside of Paris. A few years ago, at a small restaurant on the château grounds, I enjoyed a strawberry tart heaped with crème Chantilly, in the very birthplace of crème Chantilly! Lightly sweet, the original whipped cream had a cloudlike texture and an unmistakable tang—it was, in fact, whipped crème fraîche.

French Lentil Salad with Beets and Goat Cheese

Lentilles aux betteraves et chèvre

Serves 2 as a main course, or 4 as a first course

I love French lentils, with their nutty flavor and toothy bite—but in my pre–pressure cooker life, I avoided cooking them after one too many mushy batches. Happily, perfect lentils are now foolproof! This salad, inspired by the popular French food magazine Elle à Table, *pairs the legume with earthy beets, goat cheese, and a vibrant green herb vinaigrette. The combination could be described as* sain—*the French term for healthy—but it's also delicious.*

---

4 or 5 small beets, 3 to 4 inches (7.5 to 10 cm) in diameter

1 teaspoon Dijon mustard

1 tablespoon fresh lemon juice

⅓ cup (80 ml) sunflower oil

¼ cup (5 grams) chopped fresh flat-leaf parsley

¼ cup (5 grams) chopped fresh basil, chives, or dill, or a combination

2 teaspoons fine salt, plus more as desired

Freshly ground black pepper

1 cup (200 grams) French green lentils, rinsed and sorted for debris

4 ounces (115 grams) goat cheese, crumbled

1. Scrub the beets well, but take care not to pierce the skins. Place the steaming rack in the pressure cooker and add 1 cup (250 ml) water. Arrange the beets on the steaming rack. Cook on high pressure for 12 minutes.

2. While the beets are cooking, prepare the vinaigrette. In a food processor or blender, combine the mustard and lemon juice. Process to combine, then slowly add the sunflower oil and process until the mixture emulsifies. Finally, add the herbs, a pinch of salt, and pepper to taste. Process until the vinaigrette is smooth and a bright, verdant green. (The vinaigrette will retain its color for 3 to 4 hours before it begins to muddy.)

3. When the beets have finished cooking, manually release the steam. Test the beets by piercing them with a small sharp knife. If there's any resistance, close and lock the lid of the pressure cooker and allow the beets to sit in the residual heat for 3 to 5 minutes before testing again. Transfer the beets to a plate and allow them to cool.

4. Wash the inner pot of the pressure cooker. Put the lentils in the pot; add cold water to cover them by 1 inch (2.5 cm). Add the salt and stir to combine. Cook at high pressure for 10 minutes.

(continued)

5. When the beets are cool enough to handle, peel them and cut into ¼-inch-thick (6-mm) slices.

6. When the lentils have finished cooking, manually release the steam. Taste the lentils—they should be firm, but if there is too much bite, close and lock the lid of the pressure cooker and allow them to sit in the residual heat for 3 to 5 minutes before testing again.

7. Distribute the warm lentils among four plates. Arrange the beet slices on top and scatter with the crumbled goat cheese. Generously drizzle the vinaigrette over the lentils and beets in an artful manner before serving.

Salmon Rillettes

Rillettes de saumon

Serves 4–6

Rillettes are traditionally made of tough cuts of pork, duck, goose, or other meats that have been braised in their own fat until meltingly tender. Salmon rillettes are a lighter, modern alternative popular in Parisian bistros. Delicate in flavor, combining fresh and smoked salmon with butter and crème fraîche (or sour cream), they are especially quick to make when the salmon is poached in a pressure cooker. Spread on thin slices of toasted baguette, this is an elegant hors d'oeuvre or first course—especially when served with Champagne.

8 ounces (225 grams) fresh center-cut salmon fillet (skin-on)

½ cup (125 ml) white wine

4 ounces (115 grams) sliced smoked salmon, cut into fine dice

1 tablespoon fresh lemon juice, plus more as desired

2 tablespoons chopped fresh chives

2 tablespoons crème fraîche or sour cream

2 tablespoons (30 grams) unsalted butter, at room temperature

Fine salt and freshly ground black pepper

Small toasts, for serving

1. Place the steaming rack in the pressure cooker and add the wine and ½ cup (125 ml) water. Arrange the salmon on the rack, skin-side down. Cook on high pressure for 3 minutes.

2. When the salmon fillet has finished cooking, release the steam manually. Remove the fish from the pot and when it is cool enough to handle, tease the skin and dark flesh from the fillet and discard them. Flake the salmon into a large bowl. Allow to cool to room temperature.

3. Combine the flaked salmon with the chopped smoked salmon, lemon juice, chives, sour cream, and butter. Season lightly with salt and pepper, stirring to combine. Taste and adjust the seasonings, adding more salt, pepper, and/or lemon juice as desired. Chill for at least 20 minutes or up to overnight.

4. Serve with small toasts.

French Deviled Eggs

Oeufs mayonnaise

Serves 4–6

Admittedly, oeufs mayonnaise—hard-boiled eggs garnished with homemade mayonnaise—are pretty simple to make even without a multifunction cooker. But pressure-cooked hard-boiled eggs are easier to peel because the device inflates the air pocket between the egg white and the shell. This classic café starter usually features house-made mayonnaise, which French people whip up with impressive nonchalance. I use mild sunflower oil in this recipe, because it doesn't overwhelm the delicacy of the eggs. And while I know many people make mayo in the food processor, I love whipping it with a handheld mixer and anticipating the magical moment of emulsion. Serve the eggs with a few crisp leaves of lettuce and some tomato wedges.

10 large eggs

2 egg yolks

1½ teaspoons Dijon mustard

2 teaspoons fresh lemon juice, plus more as desired

¼ teaspoon fine salt, plus more as desired

Freshly ground black pepper

¾ cup sunflower oil

Fresh chives, for garnish (optional)

Butter lettuce and tomato wedges for serving (optional)

1. Place the steaming rack in the pressure cooker and add 1 cup (250 ml) water. Arrange the whole eggs on the steaming rack. Cook on low pressure for 5 minutes.

2. While the eggs are cooking, prepare the mayonnaise. In a large bowl using a handheld mixer, beat together the egg yolks, mustard, lemon juice, salt, and pepper to taste. With the mixer running, very slowly drizzle the sunflower oil, drop by drop, into the egg yolk mixture until all the oil has been completely incorporated and the mixture has emulsified into mayonnaise. Taste and add more lemon juice, salt, and pepper as desired.

3. When the eggs have finished cooking, manually release the steam. Transfer the eggs to a bowl and cover with cold water. When they're cool enough to handle, peel each egg and cut them in half lengthwise.

4. Arrange the eggs cut-side up on a large platter. Dollop a generous spoonful of mayonnaise neatly on top of each egg yolk and snip a few fresh chives over each one, if desired. Serve with a simple garnish of crisp lettuce leaves and a tomato wedge per person, if desired.

Roquefort Walnut Mini Quiches

Petites quiches au roquefort et aux noix

Serves 5

These crustless miniature quiches feature blue cheese and walnuts, which is a classic combination. In this recipe, however, the walnuts do double duty, serving as a mock "crust" that adds a crunchy bite against the soft, savory filling. Bold-flavored and rich, these quiches pair beautifully with a simple green salad.

Butter, for greasing the dishes

½ cup (20 grams) minced fresh chives, plus more for garnish

2 large eggs

¼ cup (70 grams) sour cream or crème fraîche

1 (8-ounce / 225-gram) package cream cheese (1 cup), at room temperature

¼ teaspoon fine salt

Freshly ground black pepper

2 ounces (60 grams) blue cheese, such as Roquefort

¼ cup finely chopped walnuts

1. Generously butter five 4-ounce (125-ml) oven-safe ramekins. Divide the chives among the ramekins so they cover the bottom of each dish.

2. In a large bowl, combine the eggs, sour cream, cream cheese, salt, and pepper to taste and mix well with a whisk or handheld mixer. Add the blue cheese, using the whisk or mixer to break up any large chunks.

3. Divide the blue cheese mixture among the ramekins—they should be about two-thirds full. Cover the top of each ramekin tightly with aluminum foil.

4. Place the steaming rack in the pressure cooker and add 1½ cups (375 ml) water. Arrange the ramekins on the rack, stacking them if necessary. Cook at high pressure for 5 minutes.

5. While the mini quiches are cooking, in a small skillet, toast the walnuts over medium-low heat, stirring continuously until they are lightly golden.

6. When the quiches are finished cooking, allow the pressure to release naturally. Remove the ramekins, unwrap them, and allow to cool slightly. Run a small sharp knife around the outer edge of the quiches and invert them onto individual plates. Divide the walnuts among the quiches, generously covering the surface of each quiche with nuts. Sprinkle with a few chives and serve warm, with a small green salad, if desired.

Eggplant Caviar

Caviar d'aubergine

Serves 4–6

Despite its name, this is not the prized fish roe we know as "caviar," but a dip of smoky eggplant that some believe has its roots in Lebanese cuisine. Traditionally cooked in a hot oven, the eggplant usually takes over an hour to roast—happily, the pressure cooker makes short work of the process. Spread on small toasts, this dip is popular at Parisian cocktail parties and picnics.

3 globe eggplants, about 2½ pounds (1½ kg) total
1 tomato
2 garlic cloves, chopped
1½ teaspoons fresh lemon juice, plus more as desired
½ teaspoon fine salt, plus more as desired
Freshly ground black pepper
3 tablespoons extra-virgin olive oil, plus more for drizzling
2 tablespoons chopped fresh mint and/or cilantro

1. With a small sharp knife, pierce each eggplant a few times. Using tongs, hold each eggplant over the flame of a gas stove to blacken the skins all over, rotating them frequently. (Alternatively, preheat the broiler and broil the eggplants, turning them occasionally to blacken all sides.) When they are fully charred on the outside (but still raw within), remove them from the heat.

2. Place the steaming rack in the pressure cooker and add 1 cup (250 ml) water. Arrange the charred eggplants on the rack in a single layer. Cook at high pressure for 5 minutes.

3. While the eggplants are cooking, bring a small pot of water to a boil. Put the tomato in a small bowl and cover it with the boiling water. Allow to sit for 30 seconds, then use a sharp knife to tease away the skin. Coarsely chop the tomato.

4. When the eggplants have finished cooking, manually release the steam. Use a small sharp knife to test each eggplant—the knife should slide easily to the center. If there is too much resistance, close and lock the lid and allow the eggplant to sit in the residual heat for 8 to 10 minutes before testing again.

5. Using tongs, remove the eggplants from the pressure cooker, gently squeezing them with the tongs to drain most of the excess water as you remove them. Allow them to cool slightly.

6. Slice the stem from each eggplant and use a small sharp knife to peel away the charred skin. Place the flesh in a blender or food processor and add the tomato, garlic, lemon juice, salt, pepper to taste, and the olive oil.

7. Pulse several times until the mixture is smooth. Add the fresh herbs and pulse just to combine. Taste and adjust the seasonings, adding more lemon juice and/or salt and pepper as desired.

8. Serve the dip in a shallow bowl, drizzled with additional olive oil as desired.

2

SOUPS

Les Soupes

Butternut Squash, Chestnuts, and Bacon Chips / *Potage de courge*
    butternut, châtaigne et lard fumé   26

Ribs, Stems, Roots, and Leaves / *Côtes, tiges, racines, et feuilles*   29

French Onion Soup / *Soupe à l'oignon gratinée*   30

Vegetable Soup with Basil Pistou / *Soupe au pistou*   33

French Peasant Soup / *Soupe paysanne*   36

Five Vegetable Soup / *Potage aux cinq légumes*   37

Lentils and Pork / *Petit salé aux lentilles*   38

Indian-Spiced Red Lentil Soup / *Velouté de lentilles corail*
    aux épices indiennes   41

Vietnamese Chicken Noodle Soup / *Soupe de poulet à*
    la vietnamienne   42

Chicken Stock / *Bouillon de poulet*   43

Moroccan Chickpea Soup / *Soupe de pois chiches à la marocaine*   44

Butternut Squash, Chestnuts, and Bacon Chips

Potage de courge butternut, châtaigne et lard fumé

Serves 6

Chestnuts are a hearty wintry staple in France, where they're stuffed into poultry, sweetened and pu-reed for desserts, or used to thicken and enhance soups. In the States, peeled, cooked chestnuts are sold in sous-vide packages, usually around the holidays. I love the way they heighten the faint sweetness of winter squash, but when I can't find them, I substitute potato for body and texture. For a full meal, ac-company this soup with bread and a hard cheese like Gruyère or Comté.

---

1 (2- to 3-pound / 1- to 1.5-kg) butternut squash

6½ ounces (200 grams) peeled and cooked chestnuts, or 6½ ounces (200 grams) Idaho potato, peeled and cut into 1-inch (2.5-cm) chunks

1 tablespoon olive oil

1 onion, diced

3 cups (750 ml) low-sodium chicken stock or water

Fine salt and freshly ground black pepper

2–3 slices bacon (about 2 ounces / 60 grams)

½ cup (65 grams) hulled raw pumpkin seeds

Fleur de sel (optional)

1. Cut the squash crosswise into 1-inch-thick (2.5-cm) rings. Peel each ring, then seed them (if necessary) and chop into 1-inch (2.5-cm) cubes.

2. Using the Sauté function, heat the olive oil in the pressure cooker. Add the onion and sweat until softened, about 5 minutes. Add the stock (or water) and scrape up all the brown bits at the bottom of the pot. Add the squash cubes and chestnuts (or potato). Season lightly with salt and pepper and stir to combine. Cook on high pressure for 10 minutes.

3. While the soup is cooking, in a medium skillet, cook the bacon over medium heat until very crisp. Transfer the bacon to a plate. Turn the heat to low and add the pumpkin seeds to the rendered bacon fat in the skillet. Toast until golden, about 30 seconds. Transfer the seeds to a bowl. Crumble the bacon and add it to the bowl with the toasted pumpkin seeds. Season with a pinch of fleur de sel or regular salt.

4. When the soup has finished cooking, manually release the steam. With an immersion blender, puree the soup directly in the pot until smooth. Taste and adjust the seasonings.

5. Serve garnished with the bacon and pumpkin seeds.

Ribs, Stems, Roots, and Leaves

Cardes, tiges, racines et feuilles

Serves 4

French cooks are famous for using every last scrap of food, and this recipe honors their great talent for thrift. Tough vegetable scraps like chard ribs, kale stems, and peeled broccoli trunks turn sweet and silky after a few minutes in the pressure cooker. I also use the leftover bean-cooking liquid, which gives the soup a rich, delicious, full body. Adding a handful of tender green leaves at the end ensures that the soup appears bright and pretty—and it's also a clever way to use up any leftover spinach, radish tops, or lettuce lingering in the refrigerator.

1 tablespoon olive oil

1 onion, chopped

1 Idaho potato, peeled and cubed

6 to 8 ounces (170 to 225 grams) tough vegetable scraps, such as chard ribs, peeled broccoli or cauliflower stems, kale stems, and/or cabbage leaves, coarsely chopped

3 cups (750 ml) bean-cooking liquid (such as chickpea), chicken or vegetable stock, or water

Fine salt and freshly ground black pepper

2 to 3 ounces (60 to 85 grams) tender leaves, such as spinach, parsley, and/or radish tops

1. Using the Sauté function, warm the olive oil in the pressure cooker. Add the onion and cook until softened, about 5 minutes.

2. Add the potato, tough vegetable scraps, bean-cooking liquid, and ½ teaspoon salt and stir to combine. Cook on high pressure for 5 minutes. Manually release the steam.

3. Add the tender leaves to the soup and stir until they soften completely but still retain their color, 45 seconds to 1 minute.

4. With an immersion blender, puree the soup directly in the pot until smooth. Taste and adjust the seasonings, adding more salt and pepper as desired.

French Onion Soup

Soupe à l'oignon gratinée

In France, "French onion soup"—topped with a decadent crust of golden, melted cheese—is often called simply la gratinée. Historically served at the bistros surrounding Les Halles—Paris's former central market—these days it's more often a late-night supper, slurped at weddings after a long night of dancing. Traditionally, French onion soup simmers for hours (in Mastering the Art of French Cooking, *authors Julia Child, Louisette Bertholle, and Simone Beck advise setting aside at least two and a half hours to concoct the "perfect brew"). But the intense heat of the pressure cooker—along with a pinch of baking soda and sugar to encourage the Maillard reaction that turns foods mouthwateringly golden brown— shortens the process to about thirty minutes. And though, admittedly, the texture of pressure-cooked caramelized onions is best described as a dark golden puree, their flavor is every bit as deep and richly sweet. Once the soup is capped with bubbling, golden, broiled cheese, I bet you won't notice the difference.*

---

2 pounds (900 grams) yellow onions

4 tablespoons (½ stick / 60 grams) unsalted butter

½ teaspoon baking soda

½ teaspoon sugar

¼ teaspoon fine salt, plus more as needed

½ cup (125 ml) white wine or sherry

1 quart (1 L) chicken stock

Freshly ground black pepper

1. Halve each onion through the root. Peel and cut the onion halves into ½-inch-thick (1.25-cm) slices.

2. Using the Sauté function, melt the butter in the pressure cooker. Add the onions, baking soda, sugar, and salt and stir to combine. Cook, stirring occasionally, until the onions soften and begin to release their liquid, about 3 minutes. Cook on high pressure for 20 minutes. Manually release the steam.

3. Set a colander over a large bowl. Pour in the contents of the pressure cooker, reserving the liquid. The onions will have disintegrated into a golden mass. Use a wooden spoon to press out as much liquid as possible.

4. Set the pressure cooker to the highest Sauté function and allow it to heat. Return the onion mixture to the pot. Cook, stirring frequently, until the onion mixture darkens in color and begins to stick to the bottom of the pot, about 5 minutes.

(continued)

TO SERVE

4 to 6 slices rustic bread
1 garlic clove, halved
1½ to 2 cups grated
   Gruyère or Emmenthal
   cheese

5. Add the wine and stir, scraping up any browned bits stuck to the bottom of the pot with a wooden spoon. Simmer until the wine has almost completely reduced.

6. Reduce the heat of the Sauté function to low. Add the reserved onion liquid and the stock to the onion mixture. Simmer for 8 to 10 minutes. Taste and adjust the seasonings with salt and pepper as needed.

7. To serve the soup, preheat the broiler to high. Line a baking sheet with aluminum foil. Arrange the bread on the baking sheet in a single layer. Broil each side until toasted, about 1 to 2 minutes, watching carefully to prevent burning. Rub each toast with the cut side of a garlic clove half.

8. Bring the soup to a boil and stir in ¾ cup of the grated cheese. Divide the soup among four to six oven-safe bowls. Top each bowl with a slice of toast and sprinkle with the remaining grated cheese, dividing it evenly among the bowls.

9. Carefully place the bowls on the lined baking sheet and set the baking sheet under the broiler. Broil the soup until the cheese is bubbling and golden, 1 to 3 minutes. Remove from the oven and allow to cool for a minute before serving.

Vegetable Soup with Basil Pistou

Soupe au pistou

Serves 8–10

This renowned soup of Provence is a celebration of the region's produce: basil, zucchini, and particularly fresh shell beans, which are available only in the summer months. For many Provençal cooks, it would be unthinkable to use anything else. Although nothing can match the velvety texture of fresh summer beans, dried legumes prepared speedily in the pressure cooker work in the colder months. A few years ago, I spent an entire morning helping to prepare soupe au pistou for two hundred people at a village fête in Provence. This recipe takes a fraction of the time, it's every bit as delicious—and you can make it year-round. In the winter months, when basil is expensive and hard to find, I round out a bunch with flat-leaf parsley, which adds an earthy note.

---

1 cup (200 grams) dried white beans, such as great northern, rinsed and sorted for debris (do not soak these ahead of time)

1 tablespoon olive oil

2 pounds (1 kg) zucchini

2 medium waxy potatoes

1½ pounds (750 grams) green beans, trimmed and cut into 1-inch (2.5-cm) pieces

2 teaspoons fine salt

1. Place the dried beans in the pressure cooker. Add 4 cups (1 L) water and the olive oil. Cook on high pressure for 30 minutes.

2. While the beans are cooking, peel the zucchini, leaving half the skin on in strips, and cut into 1½-inch (3.75-cm) dice. Peel the potatoes and cut into 1½-inch (3.75-cm) dice as well.

3. When the beans have finished cooking, manually release the steam. Add the zucchini, potatoes, and green beans to the pot. Stir in the salt. Cook on high pressure for 10 minutes.

4. While the soup is cooking, make the pistou: In a blender or food processor, combine the basil (and the parsley, if using), garlic, olive oil, and a pinch of salt. Blend to a smooth paste, pausing to scrape down the bowl once or twice.

5. When the soup has finished cooking, manually release the steam. Use a wooden spoon to crush a few pieces of potato and most of the zucchini against the side

(continued)

FOR THE PISTOU

4 cups (120 grams) packed
    fresh basil leaves, or a
    mix of basil and fresh
    flat-leaf parsley (see
    headnote)

2 garlic cloves

½ cup (125 ml) extra-virgin
    olive oil

Fine salt and freshly ground
    black pepper

1 cup (105 grams) elbow
    macaroni

Grated cheese, such as
    Comté, Gruyère, or
    Parmesan, for serving

of the pot to thicken the soup. Add ½ to 1 cup (125 to 250 ml) water if the soup becomes too thick.

6. Using the Sauté function, bring the soup to a simmer and add the macaroni. Cook until the macaroni is very soft, 1 to 2 minutes longer than indicated on the package. The soup will thicken considerably and can be thinned with more water, if desired.

7. Stir half the pistou into the soup and combine thoroughly. Taste and add more salt, pepper, or pistou as desired. Serve, passing the extra pistou and grated cheese at the table.

French Peasant Soup

Soupe paysanne

Serves 4–6

Simple cabbage soups have sustained the French for centuries. From soupe au chou to garbure, there exist many variations that include ingredients like cheese, ham, and stale bread, or vegetables like turnips or celery root. A slice of garlic-rubbed toast at the bottom of each bowl turns this soup into a meal.

½ to ¾ pound (500 to 750 grams) savoy cabbage (about ½ head)

1 tablespoon olive or vegetable oil

3 or 4 slices bacon (4 ounces / 115 grams), cut crosswise into ½-inch (1.25-cm) lardons

1 leek, quartered lengthwise, rinsed well, and chopped

2 potatoes, peeled and cut into ½-inch (1.25-cm) dice

2 medium carrots, halved lengthwise and cut into ½-inch (1.25-cm) pieces

2 teaspoons fine salt, plus more as desired

Freshly ground black pepper

4 to 6 slices baguette or rustic bread, for serving

1 or 2 garlic cloves, halved

1. Remove the tough outer leaves from the cabbage and slice it into four wedges. Remove and discard the core from each wedge and slice into ½-inch-thick (1.25-cm) strips.

2. Using the Sauté function, heat the oil in the pressure cooker. Add the bacon and cook until it begins to brown and the fat has rendered. Add the leek and cook, stirring, until softened.

3. Add the potatoes, carrots, cabbage, and 6 cups (1.5 L) water. Stir in the salt and season with pepper. Cook for 5 minutes on high pressure.

4. While the soup is cooking, toast the bread and rub one side of each slice with the cut side of a garlic clove half.

5. When the soup is done, manually release the steam. Taste the soup and adjust the seasonings, adding more salt and pepper as desired.

6. Place a slice of toast at the bottom of four to six shallow bowls and ladle the soup over the toast. Serve immediately.

Five Vegetable Soup

Potage aux cinq légumes

Serves 6–8

Soup—and the pressure cooker—play a significant role in French family cuisine. Soup is an easy way to eat more vegetables; it's economical, and, as a first course, it fills you up before the rest of the meal. Many of my French friends have childhood memories of soups like this one, prepared from wintry root vegetables—leeks, carrots, and potatoes are extremely common—that have been speedily softened in the pressure cooker and then lightly crushed. Sometimes the soup is served with a spoonful of crème fraîche or a pat of butter on top. This recipe—adapted from Rosi Hanson's wonderful cookbook, Recipes from the French Wine Harvest—*includes lettuce, which lends a lovely vegetal note.*

---

3 tablespoons (45 grams) butter, plus more for serving, if desired

3 leeks, quartered lengthwise, rinsed well, and coarsely chopped

1 whole head tender-leafed lettuce, such as butter, looseleaf, or oakleaf, cored and coarsely chopped

4 carrots, diced

3 potatoes, peeled and diced

2 turnips, peeled and diced

Fine salt and freshly ground black pepper

Crème fraîche or butter pats, for serving (optional)

1. Using the Sauté function, melt the butter in the pressure cooker. Add the leeks and lettuce and cook until slightly wilted, about 2 minutes.

2. Add the carrots, potatoes, and turnips, stirring to coat everything with the butter. Turn off the Sauté function. Add 3 cups (750 ml) water, season generously with salt and pepper, and stir to combine. Cook on high pressure for 10 minutes.

3. Manually release the steam. Pass the softened vegetables through a food mill fitted with a large-holed disc into a bowl. (Alternatively, you can use a potato masher to coarsely crush the vegetables or briefly blend the soup with an immersion blender directly in the pot, but don't puree the soup until smooth; it should have a rough texture.) If the soup becomes too thick, add a splash or two of water to loosen it. Taste and adjust the seasonings, adding more salt and pepper as desired.

4. Serve each bowl with a spoonful of sour cream or crème fraîche swirled through or top with a pat of butter, as desired.

Lentils and Pork

Petit salé aux lentilles

Serves 4–6

In this classic recipe, lentils are cooked with salted or smoked pork in a rich stock. This dish is traditionally served as a stew, with the lentils and meat drained of their broth. But I like to eat it as a soup, with generous spoonfuls of stock poured over. Accompanied with Dijon mustard and cornichons, this is simple, hearty comfort food. Note that though the stock takes a bit of cooking time, it's unsupervised. To make this a quick weeknight meal, start the stock before you leave the house in the morning.

1½ pounds (750 grams) pork shoulder, cut into 2-inch (5-cm) cubes

1 smoked ham hock

4 carrots, cut into ½-inch (1.25-cm)-thick rounds

1 onion, diced

3 garlic cloves, crushed

2 bay leaves

1½ cups (300 grams) French green lentils, rinsed and sorted for debris

2 teaspoons fine salt, plus more as desired

Freshly ground black pepper

Dijon mustard and cornichons, for serving (optional)

1. Put the pork shoulder, ham hock, carrots, onion, garlic, bay leaves, and 4 cups (1 L) water in the pressure cooker. Stir to combine. Cook on high pressure for 50 minutes. If you are making the full recipe right away, manually release the steam and skim off and discard any scum floating on the surface of the stock. (Alternatively, if you are making the recipe in stages, allow the pressure to release naturally and leave the stock in the pressure cooker with the Keep Warm function on; when ready to proceed, skim off and discard any scum.)

2. Add the lentils, salt, and pepper to taste to the stock in the pressure cooker. Stir to combine. Cook on high pressure for 11 minutes.

3. Manually release the steam. Taste the lentils—they should be tender, but not mushy. If there is too much bite, close and lock the lid of the pressure cooker and allow the lentils to sit in the residual heat for 5 to 10 minutes before testing again. Remove the ham hock, pull off any chunks of meat, and return the meat and collected juices to the pot with the lentils. Discard the bay leaves. Taste and adjust the seasonings, adding more salt and pepper as desired.

4. Use a slotted spoon to remove the lentils and pork from the broth, and serve in shallow bowls, ladling over the stock as desired. Serve accompanied with Dijon mustard and cornichons, if desired.

Indian-Spiced Red Lentil Soup

Velouté de lentilles corail aux épices indiennes

Serves 4–6

The daily lunch break has long been considered sacred in France, and though many people still honor the midday meal with a full, luxurious hour of three courses and wine, the "desk lunch" of the twenty-first century has begun creeping into the culture. The funny thing is, even takeout lunches are offered in three courses—a formule often consists of soup, salad, and a dessert such as yogurt. This soup, which was inspired by one of my favorite takeout spots in Paris, is perfumed with mild Indian spices and pureed until silky smooth—à la française.

1 tablespoon olive or
  vegetable oil
1 onion, chopped
3 garlic cloves, minced
2 teaspoons garam masala
1 teaspoon ground
  coriander
1 teaspoon ground turmeric
¼ teaspoon cayenne pepper
1 bay leaf
1½ cups (300 grams) red
  lentils, rinsed and sorted
  for debris
1 cup (250 ml) canned
  crushed tomatoes
2 teaspoons fine salt, plus
  more as needed
Freshly ground black
  pepper
1 (14-ounce / 400-ml) can
  coconut milk

1. Using the Sauté function, heat the vegetable oil in the pressure cooker. Add the onion and garlic and cook until softened, about 5 minutes.

2. Add the garam masala, coriander, turmeric, cayenne, and bay leaf and cook, stirring, until fragrant, about 30 seconds. Turn off the Sauté function.

3. Add the lentils, tomatoes, and 4 cups (1 L) water and stir, scraping up any browned bits from the bottom of the pot with a wooden spoon. Stir in the salt and pepper to taste. Cook on high pressure for 10 minutes.

4. Manually release the steam. Discard the bay leaf. With an immersion blender, puree the soup directly in the pot until smooth. Add the coconut milk and blend until combined. Taste and adjust the seasonings, adding more salt and pepper if desired.

Vietnamese Chicken Noodle Soup

Soupe de poulet à la vietnamienne

Serves 4

Forget French onion soup—a bowl of phô is actually the perfect way to ward off the chill of a Parisian winter day, as evidenced by the crowds packing the Vietnamese restaurants of Paris's 13th arrondissement. Traditionally, phô broth simmers for hours—but with the pressure cooker, you can start slurping within a fraction of the time.

---

1 tablespoon vegetable oil

1 onion, halved

1 (4-inch / 10-cm) piece fresh ginger, cut into ½-inch (1.25-cm) slices

1 tablespoon coriander seeds

1 (3- to 4-pound / 1.5- to 2-kg) chicken, trimmed of excess fat and cut into serving pieces

1 tablespoon raw sugar

Fine salt

Fish sauce

1 pound (450 grams) small flat rice noodles

OPTIONAL GARNISHES

1 cup (100 grams) bean sprouts; 1 cup (30 grams) fresh cilantro, mint, and/or Thai basil leaves; fish sauce; 1 lime, cut into wedges

1. Using the Sauté function, heat the vegetable oil in the pressure cooker. Add the onion, cut-sides down, and the ginger slices and cook until very brown, edging toward black, on all sides, 8 to 10 minutes.

2. Add the coriander seeds to the pot and toast until fragrant, about 45 seconds. Turn off the Sauté function.

3. Add the chicken pieces, sugar, and 2 quarts (2 L) water to the pot. Cook on high pressure for 45 minutes.

4. Allow the pressure to release naturally. Remove the chicken pieces from the broth and allow them to cool, then shred the meat (discard the bones and skin) and set it aside (you'll need 2 cups / 250 grams shredded cooked chicken; reserve any remaining chicken for another use).

5. Strain the broth through a fine-mesh sieve set over a large pot. Discard the solids, and use a spoon to skim most of the fat from the surface. Taste the broth and season it with salt and fish sauce as desired. Bring the broth to a gentle simmer over medium-low heat.

6. Cook the noodles according to the package instructions. Divide the cooked noodles among deep bowls and top each portion with about ½ cup (65 g) of the shredded chicken. Ladle over the hot broth. Garnish as desired and serve.

Chicken Stock

Bouillon de poulet

Makes about 2 quarts (2 L)

This is an embarrassing confession, but I have loathed making chicken stock for years. It takes an eternity, and the final result was always too watery and bland, especially considering the amount of time I'd invested. The first time I tried stock in the pressure cooker, I was extremely skeptical—but less than an hour later, the results completely astonished me. Not only is pressure-cooker stock easy and quick to make, its flavor is deeper and richer. To my surprise, I've become the type of person who hoards leftover chicken bones in the freezer for stock and whips out homemade broth for risotto. This staple of French cuisine really does make food taste better.

3 to 4 pounds (1.5 to 2 kg) bony chicken parts, such necks, backs, wings, and feet, or 1 cooked chicken carcass

1 onion, halved

1 carrot, coarsely chopped

1 celery stalk, coarsely chopped

1. Place the chicken, onion, carrot, and celery in the pressure cooker. Add 2 quarts (2 liters) water, making sure the volume does not exceed the pressure cooker's maximum fill line. Cook at high pressure for 45 minutes.

2. Release the pressure naturally or manually. Naturally is the tidiest method and will maintain the stock's clarity. If you're in a hurry, manually release the steam—but because there is a lot of liquid in the pressure cooker, there will be a large cloud of vapor, which can coat your kitchen surfaces with a greasy film.

3. Skim the fat from the surface of the stock. Strain the stock through a fine-mesh sieve, discarding the solids. Let cool to room temperature, portion into airtight containers, and refrigerate for 3 to 4 days or freeze for up to 6 months.

Moroccan Chickpea Soup

Soupe de pois chiches à la marocaine

Serves 4–6

North African cuisine is beloved in France, especially le couscous, a meal featuring grilled meats, vegetable stew, and semolina that frequently tops lists of France's favorite dish. This soup takes Moroccan flavors and turns them into a one-pot meal. Hearty with chickpeas and laced with harissa (a fiery chile paste), it could cheer up even the darkest winter days (of which there are many in Paris). Note that the chickpeas benefit greatly from an overnight soak, which reduces the cooking time and helps make their texture extra velvety.

---

12 ounces (340 grams) unsoaked dried chickpeas, rinsed and sorted for debris

2 tablespoons olive oil

1 onion, diced

1 celery stalk, diced

3 garlic cloves, minced

1 teaspoon ground cumin

1 teaspoon ground coriander

1 tablespoon harissa paste

2 cups (500 ml) canned crushed tomatoes

2 teaspoons fine salt, plus more if desired

Freshly ground black pepper

Chopped fresh cilantro and lemon wedges, for serving

1. Put the chickpeas in a large bowl and add cold water to cover. Soak them overnight. The next day, drain the chickpeas and set aside.

2. Using the Sauté function, heat the olive oil in the pressure cooker. Add the onion, celery, and garlic and cook until softened, about 5 minutes.

3. Stir in the cumin and coriander and cook, stirring, until fragrant, about 30 seconds. Stir in the harissa and cook for 30 seconds more. Turn off the Sauté function.

4. Add the chickpeas, tomatoes, salt, pepper to taste, and 4 cups (1 L) water and stir to combine. Cook on high pressure for 20 minutes.

5. Manually release the steam. Taste the soup, adding more salt, pepper, or harissa as desired. Serve garnished with cilantro and a squeeze of lemon.

Note: I recommend presoaking beans, especially chickpeas, which are particularly tough (see page 6). But if you do not have time to soak the chickpeas, proceed to step 3 and cook the soup on high pressure for 1 hour. Allow the pressure to release naturally for 10 minutes, then manually release the remaining steam.

CHICKEN

Le Poulet

Chicken in Red Wine Sauce / *Coq au vin* — 48

Chicken with Mushrooms and Cream / *Fricassée de poulet aux champignons* — 52

Braised Chicken with Peppers and Tomatoes / *Poulet basquaise* — 54

Chicken in Mustard Sauce / *Poulet à la moutarde* — 57

Chicken with Tarragon Sauce / *Poulet à l'estragon* — 58

Chicken Provençal / *Poulet à la provençale* — 61

Soisick's Chicken / *Poulet de Soisick* — 62

Chicken with Preserved Lemons / *Tajine de poulet aux citrons confit* — 65

Chicken in Red Wine Sauce

Coq au vin

Serves 4

While this old-fashioned country recipe traditionally uses an entire chicken—preferably a tough old bird—here I use chicken thighs, which braise beautifully in the pressure cooker. For the braising liquid, I like to use an inexpensive (don't spend more than $10), medium-bodied red wine like a Beaujolais-Villages. Buttered broad noodles are a traditional accompaniment.

---

1 to 2 tablespoons olive or vegetable oil

3 or 4 slices bacon (about 3 ounces / 85 grams), cut crosswise into ½-inch (1.25 cm) lardons

6 bone-in, skin-on chicken thighs, about 5 ounces (140 grams) each, trimmed of excess fat

1 cup (250 ml) red wine, such as Beaujolais-Villages

2 garlic cloves, minced

1 tablespoon tomato paste

½ teaspoon dried thyme

1 bay leaf

Fine salt and freshly ground black pepper

3 tablespoons (45 grams) unsalted butter

1. Using the Sauté function, heat 1 tablespoon of the olive oil in the pressure cooker. Add the bacon and cook until lightly browned, about 2 minutes. Transfer the bacon to a plate. You should have about 3 tablespoons of rendered fat left in the pressure cooker—if necessary, add an additional 1 tablespoon olive oil.

2. Dry the chicken thighs thoroughly with paper towels and add them to the pressure cooker. (You may need to do this in batches.) Cook until golden on all sides, 7 to 8 minutes. Transfer the chicken to a plate. Turn off the Sauté function.

3. Add the wine and stir, scraping any browned bits from the bottom of the pot with a wooden spoon. Add the garlic, tomato paste, thyme, and bay leaf. Season lightly with salt and pepper and stir to combine. Return the bacon and the chicken thighs to the pot, along with any juices from the plate, arranging the chicken skin-side down to absorb more color from the wine. Cook on high pressure for 25 minutes.

4. While the chicken cooks, in a medium skillet, melt 2 tablespoons (30 grams) of the butter over medium-high heat until foamy. When the foam has started to subside, add the mushrooms and cook, shaking the pan frequently, until the mushrooms are tender and lightly browned, about 5 minutes. Season lightly with salt and pepper. Remove from the heat and allow to cool.

(continued)

½ pound (250 grams)
   button mushrooms,
   quartered if large
1 tablespoon all-purpose
   flour
¼ to ½ cup (60 to 120
   ml) low-sodium chicken
   stock (optional)
Buttered broad noodles, for
   serving

5. In a small bowl, mash the flour into the remaining 1 tablespoon (15 grams) butter until it forms a smooth paste (this is the *beurre manié*).

6. When the chicken has finished cooking, manually release the steam. Transfer the chicken to a plate, leaving the liquid in the pot. Discard the bay leaf.

7. Using the Sauté function, bring the cooking liquid to a simmer. With a wire whisk, beat in the *beurre manié* until the sauce becomes glossy and coats the back of a spoon. If the sauce becomes too thick, add the stock, starting with 1 tablespoon. Taste and adjust the seasonings, adding more salt and pepper as desired.

8. Return the chicken, along with any juices from the plate, and mushrooms to the pressure cooker and heat them through in the sauce. Serve with buttered broad noodles.

BEURRE MANIÉ

Sauces are one of the pressure cooker's weak points, as liquid cannot evaporate and reduce while it is sealed. Flour or other starch added to the pressure cooker before sealing could burn on the bottom or clog the vent holes. Given these factors, the sauce of a dish braised in the pressure cooker is thin. It's up to you, then, to thicken it.

A classic *beurre manié*—or "kneaded butter"—is the perfect solution. Composed of equal parts flour and butter that have been mashed together, the paste is whisked into hot braising liquid at the end of the cooking time, turning the sauce thick and glossy, without lumps.

Beurre manié is extremely easy to make—just use a fork to mash butter and flour together on a plate. But to save time, you can prepare a large quantity in the food processor. Divide it into 1-tablespoon portions and store them in the freezer. When you need to thicken a sauce, simply throw a frozen lump into your boiling braising liquid and whisk away.

Chicken with Mushrooms and Cream

Fricassée de poulet aux champignons

Serves 4

A fricassée is a quintessentially French recipe in which morsels of poultry are gently braised in a lightly thickened stock. With the magic of the pressure cooker, this dish becomes a quick weeknight meal. This recipe uses boneless, skinless chicken thighs (boneless, skinless turkey thighs are also delicious). Because there is flour in the cooking liquid, it's important to release the pressure in the pot naturally—a quick release could clog the vent holes. Serve this dish with rice or mashed potatoes; alternatively, you could use it as the filling for chicken potpie, scooped into a baking dish and topped with a sheet of prepared puff pastry.

---

3 tablespoons (45 grams) unsalted butter

2 pounds (1 kg) boneless, skinless chicken thighs, trimmed of fat and cut into 1- to 2-inch (3- to 5-cm) pieces

1 large onion, diced

2 tablespoons all-purpose flour

½ pound (250 grams) button mushrooms, cut into ¼-inch-thick (6-mm) slices

½ teaspoon dried thyme

¼ cup (75 ml) chicken stock

Fine salt and freshly ground black pepper

3 tablespoons sour cream or crème fraîche

1. Using the Sauté function, melt the butter in the pressure cooker. Add the chicken thighs and cook until the pieces are lightly colored, about 3 minutes. Turn off the Sauté function.

2. Add the onion, flour, mushrooms, thyme, stock, 1 teaspoon salt, and some pepper to the pressure cooker and stir to combine. Cook on high pressure for 4 minutes.

3. Allow the pressure to release naturally. Using the Sauté function, bring the cooking liquid to a boil and cook until the sauce has reduced by a third, about 8 to 10 minutes. Turn off the Sauté function.

4. With a whisk, beat in the sour cream until fully incorporated. Taste the sauce and adjust the seasonings before serving.

Braised Chicken with Peppers and Tomatoes

Poulet basquaise

Serves 4

This bright dish from southwestern France combines peppers, tomatoes, and piment d'Espelette, the Basque region's beloved chile powder, which is made from sun-dried local peppers and has a rich, deep, almost smoky flavor and subtle heat. If you can't find piment d'Espelette, substitute sweet paprika. This dish is traditionally served with rice.

2 tablespoons olive oil

6 bone-in, skin-on chicken thighs, about 5 ounces (140 grams) each, trimmed of excess fat

1 medium onion, diced

1 pound (500 grams) red bell peppers, cut into ¼-inch-thick (6-mm) slices

2 garlic cloves, thinly sliced

¾ cup (180 ml) canned whole tomatoes, lightly crushed by hand

½ teaspoon sugar, plus more as needed

½ teaspoon *piment d'Es-pelette* or sweet paprika, plus more as needed

Fine salt and freshly ground black pepper

Cooked long-grain rice, for serving

1. Using the Sauté function, heat the olive oil in the pressure cooker. Dry the chicken thighs with paper towels and add them to the pressure cooker. (You may need to do this in batches.) Cook until golden brown on all sides, about 7 to 8 minutes. Transfer the chicken to a plate.

2. Add the onion and bell peppers to the pot and cook until softened, 2 to 3 minutes, stirring and scraping up any browned bits from the bottom of the pot with a wooden spoon. Add the garlic and cook until fragrant, about 1 minute. Turn off the Sauté function.

3. Add the tomatoes, sugar, and *piment d'Espelette* to the pressure cooker. Season lightly with salt and black pepper and stir to combine.

4. Return the chicken to the pot, along with any juices from the plate, nestling it into the sauce skin-side down. Cook on high pressure for 25 minutes.

5. Manually release the steam. Transfer the chicken to a plate, leaving the vegetables and their liquid in the pot. Using the Sauté function, bring the cooking liquid to a rapid boil. Cook, stirring frequently, until most of the liquid has evaporated, about 10 minutes. Taste and adjust the seasonings, adding more sugar, *piment d'Espelette*, and/or salt and black pepper as needed.

6. Return the chicken to the pot, along with any juices from the plate, nestling it into the sauce, and heat it through. Serve with long-grained rice, like basmati.

Chicken in Mustard Sauce

Poulet à la moutarde

Serves 4

A French country classic, this recipe uses two types of Dijon mustard, whole-grain and smooth, to create a tangy sauce that pairs well with chicken—or, if you're feeling particularly bold, it's also delicious with rabbit. Serve with buttered broad noodles.

2 tablespoons olive or vegetable oil

6 bone-in, skin-on chicken thighs and/or chicken legs, about 3 pounds (1.5 kg) total, trimmed of excess fat

1 medium onion, diced

½ cup (125 ml) white wine

½ cup (125 ml) chicken stock

Fine salt and freshly ground black pepper

3 tablespoons smooth Dijon mustard

1 tablespoon whole-grain Dijon mustard

3 tablespoons sour cream or crème fraîche

1. Using the Sauté function, heat the olive oil in the pressure cooker. Dry the chicken thoroughly with paper towels and add it to the pot. (You may need to do this in batches.) Cook until golden brown on all sides, about 7 to 8 minutes. Transfer the chicken to a plate.

2. Add the onion to the pot and cook until softened, about 5 minutes. Add the stock and the wine and stir, scraping up any browned bits from the bottom of the pot with a wooden spoon. Return the chicken to the pot along with any juices from the plate, and season lightly with salt and pepper. Cook on high pressure for 25 minutes.

3. Manually release the steam. Transfer the chicken to a plate, leaving the liquid in the pot. Using the Sauté function, bring the cooking liquid to a rapid boil and cook, stirring frequently, until it has reduced by half. Turn off the Sauté function and whisk in the smooth and whole-grain mustards and the sour cream. Taste the sauce and add more salt and pepper as desired.

4. Return the chicken along with any juices from the plate to the sauce in the pressure cooker and gently warm it through before serving.

Chicken with Tarragon Sauce

Poulet à l'estragon

Serves 4

Along with parsley, chervil, and chives, tarragon is considered one of the four fines herbes of French cuisine. It has a savory, licorice perfume that is, to me, quintessentially français. Even a small pinch of fresh tarragon adds an undeniable French twist to a simple omelet or vinaigrette. This dish, which combines white wine, cream, and a generous amount of tarragon, will make you feel like you're dining in a Paris bistro.

1 tablespoon (15 grams) unsalted butter

1 tablespoon olive oil

6 bone-in, skin-on chicken thighs and/or chicken legs, about 3 pounds (1.5 kg) total, trimmed of excess fat

2 shallots, diced

½ cup (125 ml) white wine

½ cup (125 ml) chicken stock

2 tablespoons chopped fresh tarragon, plus whole leaves for garnish

Salt and freshly ground black pepper

3 tablespoons sour cream or crème fraîche

1. Using the Sauté function, heat the butter and olive oil in the pressure cooker. Dry the chicken thoroughly with paper towels and add it to the pot. (You may need to do this in batches.) Cook until golden brown on all sides, about 7 to 8 minutes. Transfer the chicken to a plate.

2. Add the shallots to the pot and cook until softened, about 3 minutes. Add the broth and the wine and stir, scraping up any browned bits from the bottom of the pot with a wooden spoon. Add the tarragon and return the chicken to the pot, along with any juices from the plate, stirring to combine. Season lightly with salt and pepper. Cook on high pressure for 25 minutes.

3. Manually release the steam. Transfer the chicken to a plate, leaving the liquid in the pot. Using the Sauté function, bring the cooking liquid to a rapid boil and cook, stirring frequently, until reduced by half. Turn off the Sauté function. Add the sour cream and whisk continuously as the sauce thickens. Taste and add more salt and pepper as desired.

4. Return the chicken to the sauce along with any juices from the plate and gently warm it through. Serve sprinkled with tarragon leaves.

Chicken Provençal

Poulet à la provençale

Serves 4

Anchovies, olives, and tomato paste evoke the sunny South of France in this quick-and-easy dish that packs a lot of flavor into a small amount of time and effort.

---

2 tablespoons olive oil

6 bone-in, skin-on chicken thighs and/or chicken legs, about 3 pounds (1.5 kg) total, trimmed of excess fat

2 garlic cloves, thinly sliced

2 anchovies

2 tablespoons natural (no-salt-added) tomato paste

1 cup (250 ml) red wine

Freshly ground black pepper

½ cup (75 grams) canned pitted black olives

½ teaspoon sugar, plus more as desired

Fine salt

Chopped fresh flat-leaf parsley, for garnish (optional)

1. Using the Sauté function, heat the olive oil in the pressure cooker. Dry the chicken thoroughly with paper towels and add it to the pot. (You may need to do this in batches.) Cook until golden brown on all sides, about 7 to 8 minutes. Transfer the chicken to a plate.

2. Add the garlic, anchovies, and 1 tablespoon of the tomato paste to the pot and cook until fragrant, about 1 minute. Add the wine and stir, scraping up any browned bits from the bottom of the pot with a wooden spoon. Turn off the Sauté function. Return the chicken to the pot, along with any juices from the plate. Season lightly with pepper, but do not add salt right now, as the anchovies are quite salty. Cook on high pressure for 25 minutes.

3. Manually release the steam. Transfer the chicken to a plate, leaving the liquid in the pot. Add the olives to the cooking liquid. Using the Sauté function, bring the liquid to a rapid boil and cook, stirring frequently, until reduced by half. Add the sugar and whisk in the remaining 1 tablespoon tomato paste. Cook until the sauce thickens slightly. Taste and season with salt, more sugar, and pepper as desired.

4. Return the chicken to the sauce along with any juices from the plate and warm it through. Serve sprinkled with parsley, if desired.

Soisick's Chicken

Poulet de Soisick

Serves 4

Soisick is the French mother-in-law of my friend Erin—and she is also a pressure cooker aficionado. Her chicken is beloved in the family, and often appears on the Sunday lunch table. "Nothing is more simple," she says. This recipe is a cross between poule au pot—a whole poached chicken—and a rotisserie bird. (This is not a roast chicken, and if you are hoping for crackling crisp skin, you will be disappointed.) There is something addictive about this simple chicken, with its deep, pure flavor and richly flavored jus—it is true French comfort food.

---

1 (3- to 4-pound / 1.5- to 2-kg) whole chicken

Fine salt and freshly ground black pepper

2 tablespoons olive or vegetable oil

1 onion, sliced

¼ cup (60 ml) dry white wine

1 pound (500 grams) tomatoes, coarsely chopped

1½ pounds (750 grams) potatoes, peeled and cut into 2-inch (5-cm) chunks

3 tablespoons (45 grams) unsalted butter, melted

1. Trim the excess fat and skin from the chicken. Dry the chicken with paper towels and season it generously with salt and pepper.

2. Using the Sauté function, heat the olive oil in the pressure cooker. Place the chicken breast-side down in the pot and brown it on all sides, 7 to 9 minutes per side. Using tongs, carefully transfer the chicken to a large plate or platter.

3. Add the onion to the pot and cook until softened, about 3 minutes. Add the wine and scrape up all the browned bits from the bottom with a wooden spoon. Cook until the wine has almost fully evaporated.

4. Add the tomatoes, 1½ teaspoons of salt, and some pepper to the pot, stirring to combine. Return the chicken to the pot, along with any juices from the plate, and arrange the potatoes around it. Cook on high pressure for 15 minutes.

5. While the chicken is cooking, preheat the oven to broil. Line a baking sheet with aluminum foil.

6. When the chicken has finished cooking, allow the pressure to release naturally for 10 minutes, then manually release the steam. Leaving the liquid in the pot,

(continued)

carefully transfer the chicken and potatoes to the prepared baking sheet and drizzle them with the melted butter. Slide the baking sheet into the oven and broil to lightly brown the chicken and potatoes, about 5 minutes.

7. Meanwhile, using the Sauté function, bring the cooking liquid to a rapid boil and cook until it has reduced by a third, about 10 minutes. Strain the cooking liquid—or jus—through a fine-mesh sieve into a bowl; discard the solids.

8. Pour the *jus* into a sauceboat. Serve the chicken and potatoes, passing the *jus* at the table.

Note: There will be quite a lot of cooking liquid, which in France is served simply as *jus*, unadorned. It is delicious spooned lightly over the chicken and potatoes.

Chicken with Preserved Lemons

Tajine de poulet aux citrons confits

Serves 4

When I was twelve or thirteen, my parents and I went on a summer vacation to Provence—and that was the moment I started falling in love with France. One night, we had dinner at the home of some friends of friends, an Algerian family who had moved to a suburb of Marseille. The wife made an exotic (to us) dish of braised chicken and preserved lemons, full of salty, tangy, bitter savor. It was the first tagine we had ever tasted. My dad took copious notes and began making it at home in California—it has since become a family favorite. A few months ago, my father found his original recipe notes, and I adapted them for the pressure cooker.

2 tablespoons olive oil

6 bone-in, skin-on chicken thighs and/or chicken legs, about 3 pounds (1.5 kg) total, trimmed of excess fat

2 medium onions, cut into wedges

1 garlic clove, thinly sliced

3 medium tomatoes (about 1 pound / 500 grams), cut into wedges

5 fresh cilantro sprigs (leaves and stems), plus chopped leaves for garnish, as desired

Pinch of saffron

1 preserved lemon (recipe follows), cut into wedges

1. Using the Sauté function, heat the olive oil in the pressure cooker. Dry the chicken with paper towels and add it to the pot. (You may need to do this in batches.) Cook until golden brown on all sides, about 7 to 8 minutes. Transfer the chicken to a plate.

2. Add the onions to the pressure cooker and cook until the edges begin to turn golden, 4 to 5 minutes. Add 1 cup (250 ml) water and scrape up any browned bits from the bottom of the pot with a wooden spoon. Add the garlic, tomatoes, cilantro, saffron, and preserved lemon. Return the chicken to the pot, along with any collected juices from the plate. Season lightly with salt and pepper. Cook at high pressure for 25 minutes.

3. While the chicken is cooking, place the couscous and ½ teaspoon salt in a large bowl and stir to combine.

4. When the chicken has finished cooking, manually release the steam. Transfer the chicken to a plate, leaving the liquid in the pot. Using the Sauté function, bring

(continued)

Fine salt and freshly ground
  black pepper
1 cup couscous

the cooking liquid to a rapid boil. Remove 1 cup (250 ml) of the liquid from the pressure cooker and stir it into the couscous. Cover the bowl with a plate and allow to stand for 10 minutes. Meanwhile, taste the braising liquid and adjust the seasonings, adding more salt and pepper as desired.

5. Return the chicken to the sauce in the pressure cooker and heat through. Serve the chicken with the sauce, garnished with chopped cilantro, if desired, and accompanied by the couscous.

Preserved Lemons

4 organic lemons
¼ cup kosher salt

SPECIAL EQUIPMENT
1 glass jar, just large
  enough to hold 4 lemons,
  with a lid

1. Wash the lemons. Cut them into quarters, but not all the way through, so that the pieces remain attached at the stem end.

2. Generously stuff each lemon with salt. Stuff them into the jar, pressing down to fit them all inside. Seal the jar.

3. Leave the lemons at room temperature for 1 week, during which time they will soften and release some of their juices. Open the jar each day to release any pent-up gases.

4. After a week, reseal the jar and store it in the fridge for a month before using the preserved lemons. They will keep for 6 months, stored in the refrigerator.

Note: If you make preserved lemons frequently, save the juice that collects at the bottom of the jar and use it to inoculate your next batch. It will greatly speed up the softening process.

4

FISH AND SHELLFISH
Les Poissons et les Fruits de Mer

Mussels Steamed with White Wine, Garlic, and Parsley

Moules marinières

Serves 4

Mussels have been cultivated in France since the thirteenth century, and the most common way of preparing them is one of the simplest: à la marinière means "as the sailors eat them"—steamed with garlic, parsley, and white wine. The pressure cooker makes cooking mussels a snap—the intense, uniform temperature ensures perfection every time.

---

2 pounds (1 kg) mussels

4 tablespoons (½ stick / 60 grams) unsalted butter

2 shallots, minced

3 garlic cloves, thinly sliced

1 cup (250 ml) dry white wine

Freshly ground black pepper

¼ cup (10 grams) chopped fresh flat-leaf parsley

Fine salt

Crusty bread, for serving

1. Rinse and sort the mussels in cold water, scrubbing them well and pulling out the beard. Discard any mussels with broken shells. If there are any open mussels, give them a sharp tap—if they do not close, throw them away (they are dead).

2. Using the Sauté function, melt the butter in the pressure cooker. Add the shallots and garlic and cook until slightly softened, about 1 minute. Add the wine and a generous sprinkle of pepper and simmer until the shallots and garlic are tender, about 5 minutes. Turn off the Sauté function.

3. Add the mussels to the pot. Cook on low pressure for 1 minute. Manually release the steam.

4. Stir the mussels, discarding any that remain closed. Add the parsley and stir to distribute.

5. Taste the broth that has collected at the bottom of the pot and season it with salt and pepper, as desired.

6. Divide the mussels among four individual shallow bowls and spoon the broth over the top. Serve immediately, with crusty bread.

Note: The mussels cook at low pressure, so make sure to adjust the cooker.

Potato Salad with Mussels

Salade de pommes de terre aux moules

Serves 4

A salad of mussels and potatoes is a classic Mediterranean preparation, popular in southern France and Spain. You can use any quantity of mussels in this dish—this is a great way to use up any leftovers from moules marinières (page 70)—there's no need to be exact. This makes a lovely composed salad, arranged prettily on a bed of lettuce, with tomatoes, hard-boiled eggs, black olives, capers, anchovies, or whatever strikes your fancy.

2 pounds (1 kg) mussels

1 cup (250 ml) dry white wine

½ cup (60 grams) finely chopped yellow onion

Zest of 1 lemon

3 tablespoons fresh lemon juice

½ teaspoon fine salt, plus more as desired

¼ teaspoon sugar

1 pound (500 grams) waxy potatoes, like Yukon Gold

¼ cup (125 ml) extra-virgin olive oil

¼ cup (10 grams) chopped fresh flat-leaf parsley

Freshly ground black pepper

1. Rinse and sort the mussels in cold water, scrubbing them well and pulling out the beard. Discard any mussels with broken shells. If there are any open mussels, give them a sharp tap—if they do not close, throw them away (they are dead).

2. Put the mussels and wine in the pressure cooker. Cook on low pressure for 1 minute.

3. While the mussels are cooking, in a large bowl, stir together the chopped onion, lemon zest, lemon juice, salt, and sugar.

4. When the mussels have finished cooking, manually release the steam. Remove the mussels from the pot, discarding any that remain closed, and set aside in a bowl to cool. (Save the broth for another use.)

5. Wash the inner pot of the pressure cooker. Place the steaming rack inside and add 1 cup (250 ml) water. Arrange the potatoes on the rack. Adjust the settings and cook on high pressure for 13 minutes.

6. While the potatoes are cooking, remove the cooled mussels from their shells (discard the shells).

7. When the potatoes are finished cooking, manually release the steam. Remove the potatoes from the pot and set aside until cool enough to handle. Peel the potatoes and cut them into bite-size (1-inch / 2.5-cm) slices.

8. Whisk the olive oil into the onion-lemon mixture in the large bowl to create a vinaigrette. Add the potatoes, mussels, and parsley and stir gently to combine. Taste and add pepper and more salt as desired. Serve warm or at room temperature.

Rolled Fillets of Sole with Herbed Bread Crumbs

Roulés de sole croustillant

Serves 4

Sole is one of my favorite fish, but it can be expensive or difficult to find, especially out of season. Happily, modern fish-freezing technology means that it is now often caught wild and sold frozen—a sustainable practice that also maintains the fish's texture, quality, and nutrients. I used to make this dish in the oven, before I discovered that the pressure cooker keeps the sole fillets beautifully moist and tender. The bread crumbs offer a crunchy, flavorful counterpoint, and I also like to add a pinch of dried chile flakes for an extra spark. Boiled new potatoes are a good accompaniment.

---

1 tablespoon (15 grams) salted butter, at room temperature

2 tablespoons white wine

8 sole fillets, about 2 ounces (55 grams) each (about 1 pound / 454 grams total)

Fine salt and freshly ground black pepper

2 tablespoons olive oil

1 garlic clove, minced

½ cup (25 grams) panko bread crumbs

2 tablespoons chopped fresh flat-leaf parsley, plus more for garnish

1 tablespoon lemon zest

Pinch of dried chile flakes (optional)

1. Spread the butter over the bottom of an 8-inch (20-cm) round baking dish. Add the wine to the dish.

2. Lightly season the sole fillets with salt and black pepper. Roll each fillet starting from one narrow end and secure it with a toothpick. Arrange the rolls in the prepared baking dish. Cover tightly with aluminum foil.

3. Place the steaming rack in the pressure cooker and add 1½ cups (375 ml) water. Place the baking dish on the rack. Cook on high pressure for 3 minutes.

4. While the fish is cooking, in a medium skillet, heat the olive oil over medium heat. Add the garlic and stir until fragrant. Add the bread crumbs, parsley, lemon zest, chile flakes (if using), a generous pinch of fleur de sel, and black pepper to taste. Toast the bread crumbs, stirring frequently, until they turn golden. Remove from the heat.

5. When the fish has finished cooking, manually release the steam. Remove the baking dish from the pressure cooker and carefully unwrap it. Remove the toothpicks from the rolled fish.

(continued)

Fleur de sel

Lemon wedges, for serving

SPECIAL EQUIPMENT

8-inch (20-cm) round baking dish (without handles)

6. Divide the bread crumbs among the rolled fish fillets, mounding them on top. (Don't worry if some of the crumbs fall into the sauce in the baking dish—they will thicken it slightly.) Sprinkle with parsley, and serve immediately, with wedges of lemon alongside.

Fish en Papillote with Chard, Mushrooms, and Soy-Butter Broth

Poisson en papillote aux blettes, champignons et bouillon de sauce soja au beurre

Serves 4

I love the method of cooking en papillote—small packets of food in parchment paper or foil, unwrapped like gifts at the table. This recipe combines Asian and French flavors in homage to Jean-Georges Vongerichten.

½ pound (250 grams) Swiss chard
½ pound (250 grams) button mushrooms
4 (5- to 6-ounce / 140- to 170-gram) fillets turbot, halibut, flounder, or lemon sole
2 tablespoons (30 grams) unsalted butter
2 green onions, cut into thin strips about 2 inches (5 cm) in length
2 tablespoons soy sauce
2 tablespoons dry sherry
Freshly ground black pepper
Lemon wedges, for serving

1. Remove the tough center stalks from the chard (save them for the Ribs, Stems, Roots, Leaves soup on page 29). Chop the leaves into ribbons. Cut the mushrooms into ¼-inch-thick (6-mm) slices. Tear off four rectangles of aluminum foil, about 12 x 16 inches (30 x 40 cm).

2. Divide the chard among the foil rectangles. Repeat with the mushrooms, arranging them on top of the chard. Place a fish fillet on each mound of vegetables. Dot each fillet with ½ tablespoon of the butter. Divide the green onions among the packets, placing them on top of each piece of fish.

3. Sprinkle ½ tablespoon of the soy sauce over each fish fillet, followed by ½ tablespoon of the sherry. Season with pepper. Bring the edges of the foil together over the fish and vegetables and crimp the edges to seal tightly so that everything is completely enclosed within the foil.

4. Place the steaming rack in the pressure cooker and add 1½ cups (375 ml) water. Place the foil packets on the rack, stacking them if necessary. Cook on high pressure for 10 minutes.

5. Manually release steam. Remove the packets and set on individual plates. Serve immediately, opening the packets at the table. Squeeze over lemon, as desired.

Salmon with Melted Leeks and Whole-Grain Mustard

Saumon à la fondue de poireaux et moutarde à l'ancienne

Serves 4

Creamy melted leeks are a staple of northern France, tucked into buckwheat galettes in Brittany, or folded into omelets. Here they are a delicious side dish to poached salmon—while a dollop of whole-grain Dijon mustard adds a delicate, caviar-like crunch. This dish looks elegant, but the leeks and salmon cook together under pressure, making this a quick one-pot meal.

---

3 leeks (about 1½ pounds / 750 grams)

4 tablespoons (½ stick / 60 grams) unsalted butter

1 teaspoon fine salt, plus more as desired

Freshly ground black pepper

4 (5- to 6-ounce / 140- to 170-gram) salmon fillets

3 tablespoons sour cream or crème fraîche

Whole-grain Dijon mustard, for serving

Fresh dill sprigs, for garnish

1. Halve the leeks lengthwise, rinse them well to remove any grit, and chop them into ½-inch-thick (1.5-cm) semicircles.

2. Using the Sauté function, melt the butter in the pressure cooker. Add the leeks and cook until slightly softened, 2 to 3 minutes. Season with the salt and pepper to taste. Turn off the Sauté function.

3. Lightly season the salmon fillets with salt and pepper. Place the steaming rack in the pressure cooker on top of the leeks, making sure that all the legs touch the bottom. Arrange the salmon fillets skin-side down on the rack. Cook on high pressure for 1 minute. Manually release the steam.

4. Remove the salmon fillets from the pressure cooker by lifting out the steaming rack; set it on a plate. Loosely tent the salmon with a piece of aluminum foil.

5. Using the Sauté function, bring the leeks to a boil and cook until almost all the liquid has evaporated, 6 to 8 minutes. Turn off the Sauté function. Add the sour cream and stir to combine. Taste the leeks and adjust the seasonings, adding more salt and pepper as desired.

6. Divide the leeks evenly among four plates. Nestle a salmon fillet on top of each bed of leeks. Place a generous dollop of mustard on each fillet. Garnish with dill sprigs and serve immediately.

Poached Cod with Tomato, Fennel, and Saffron Broth

Cabillaud poché au bouillon de tomate, fenouil et safran

Serves 4

Bouillabaisse, a once-humble fish stew of the poor, now has its own charter to protect its integrity. True bouillabaisse uses only Mediterranean seafood such as rockfish, St-Pierre, monkfish, and conger eel—ingredients that can be difficult to find outside of the region. Inspired by the original, this recipe combines readily available cod with Provençal flavors like fennel, tomatoes, and saffron.

2 tablespoons olive oil

1 medium fennel bulb, trimmed and cut into ½-inch (1.25-cm) dice, fronds reserved

3 garlic cloves, thinly sliced

1 pound (500 grams) tomatoes, coarsely chopped

1 teaspoon saffron

1½ teaspoons fine salt

Freshly ground black pepper

4 (5- to 6-ounce / 140- to 170-gram) cod fillets

1. Using the Sauté function, heat the olive oil in the pressure cooker. Add the fennel and garlic and cook until slightly softened, 2 to 3 minutes. Add the tomatoes, saffron, and 1 cup (250 ml) water and bring to a simmer. Season with the salt and pepper to taste. Turn off the Sauté function. Cook on high pressure for 4 minutes.

2. While the tomato broth is cooking, lightly season the cod fillets with salt and pepper.

3. When the broth has finished cooking, manually release the steam. Working quickly, place the cod fillets in the pot on top of the tomato-fennel broth. Cook on high pressure for 2 minutes. Allow the pressure to release naturally for 5 minutes, then manually release the steam. The cod should be opaque to the middle and beginning to flake. If it is not cooked through, close and lock the lid and allow the fillets to sit in the residual heat for 3 to 5 minutes before testing again.

4. Transfer the cod to individual shallow bowls. Taste the broth and season with more salt and pepper as desired. Spoon the broth and vegetables over each fillet. Garnish with fennel fronds, and serve.

Poached Salmon with Olive and Almond Tapenade

Saumon poché, tapenade d'olives et amandes

Serves 4

In Provence, recipes for homemade tapenade are kept close to the vest. For years, I've been hoping (in vain) that a friend's mother-in-law would reveal her secrets—but in the meantime, I've been forced to create my own. It's almost as good, and it pairs nicely with poached salmon for a simple, light supper. For this recipe, I like cooking a single large fillet of salmon and serving it family-style, with the tapenade dolloped on top.

1 (1- to 1½-pound / 500- to 750-gram) center-cut salmon fillet

2 tablespoons capers, preferably salt-packed, rinsed and squeezed dry

¾ cup (105 grams) blanched slivered almonds

3 anchovy fillets

1 garlic clove

½ cup (15 grams) fresh flat-leaf parsley leaves

Juice of 1 lemon

2 cups (8 ounces / 230 grams) pitted green olives

¼ cup (60 ml) olive oil

Fine salt and freshly ground black pepper

Fleur de sel (optional)

Lemon wedges, for serving

1. Place the steaming rack in the pressure cooker and add 1 cup (250 ml) water. Arrange the salmon on the rack, skin-side down. Cook on high pressure for 6 minutes.

2. While the salmon is cooking, in a food processor or blender, combine the capers, almonds, anchovies, garlic, parsley, and lemon juice and process until roughly chopped and combined. Add the olives and olive oil and pulse a few times until the mixture becomes a chunky paste—some small bits of almond will remain; they add texture. Taste and season with salt and pepper as desired.

3. When the salmon fillet has finished cooking, release the steam manually. Remove the salmon from the pressure cooker and place it on a platter. Season it lightly with fleur de sel (if using) or regular salt, and pepper. Spoon about ¾ cup (180 ml) of the tapenade artfully on top of the salmon. Serve family-style, passing additional tapenade and lemon wedges at the table.

Fish Fillets Poached in White Wine with Mushrooms

Filets de poisson à la Bercy aux champignons

Serves 4

Bercy was once home to the largest wine market in Europe—and, as a result, its name is synonymous with dishes cooked in wine. In this recipe, delicate fillets of fish are poached in white wine, and the liquid is turned into a creamy sauce. Note that the fish filets are pressure cooked for zero minutes, which means the cooker is brought to pressure and then the steam is immediately released.

---

2 tablespoons minced shallot

½ cup (125 ml) white wine

½ cup (125 ml) unsalted fish or chicken stock

4 (5- to 6-ounce / 140- to 170-gram) turbot, halibut, flounder, or lemon sole fillets

Fine salt and freshly ground black pepper

2 tablespoons (30 grams) unsalted butter

½ pound (250 grams) brown button mushrooms, sliced

1 tablespoon all-purpose flour

2 tablespoons sour cream or crème fraîche

A few drops of fresh lemon juice (optional)

Chopped fresh parsley

1. Place the shallot, wine, and stock in the pressure cooker and stir to combine. Lightly season the fish fillets with salt and pepper and arrange them in the pressure cooker, overlapping them slightly if necessary. Cook on high pressure for 0 minutes (see page xxii), bringing the cooker to pressure before immediately releasing the steam.

2. While the fish is cooking, in a large skillet, melt 1 tablespoon (15 grams) of the butter over medium-high heat until foamy. When the foam starts to subside, add the mushrooms and cook until softened, 1 to 2 minutes. Season lightly with salt and pepper and remove from the heat.

3. In a small bowl, mash the flour into the remaining 1 tablespoon (15 grams) butter until it forms a smooth paste (this is the beurre manié).

4. When the fish has finished cooking, manually release the steam. Transfer the fillets to a plate, leaving the liquid in the pot. Using the Sauté function, bring the poaching liquid to a brisk simmer. With a wire whisk, beat the beurre manié into the liquid until the sauce thickens slightly. Add the cream, whisking to combine. Taste and adjust the seasonings, adding the lemon juice and/or more salt and pepper as desired.

5. Return the fish fillets to the sauce and gently warm everything through. Serve immediately, garnished with parsley, if desired.

Halibut with Beurre Blanc, Tarragon, and Capers

Poisson au beurre blanc, estragon et câpres

Serves 4

Beurre blanc means "white butter"—and though this sauce uses a lot of its signature ingredient, it has a lovely, light, pleasantly acidic flavor that works especially well with tarragon. Beurre blanc is an emulsion of reduced vinegar and butter—and while that sounds intimidating, it's actually easy to whip up in the time the fish cooks. To help the sauce emulsify, make sure your butter is well chilled.

---

4 (5- to 6-ounce / 140- to 170-gram) halibut fillets

3 tablespoons white wine vinegar

3 tablespoons white wine

1 tablespoon finely minced shallot

Fine salt and freshly ground black pepper

10 tablespoons (150 grams) chilled unsalted butter

1 tablespoon chopped fresh tarragon

1 tablespoon capers, rinsed and squeezed dry

1. Place the steaming rack in the pressure cooker and add 1 cup (250 ml) water. Arrange the fish fillets on the rack. Cook on high pressure for 0 minutes (see page xxii), bringing the cooker to pressure before immediately releasing the steam.

2. While the fish is cooking, in a small saucepan, combine the vinegar, wine, shallot, and 2 tablespoons (30 grams) of the butter. Bring to a rapid boil over medium heat and cook until the liquid has reduced by about half. Meanwhile, cut the remaining 8 tablespoons (120 grams) chilled butter into ½-inch (1.25-cm) cubes.

3. When the fish has finished cooking, release the steam manually. Transfer each fillet to an individual plate and lightly season with salt and pepper. Cover loosely with foil to keep warm.

4. When the vinegar-wine mixture has finished reducing, remove the saucepan from the heat. Using a wire whisk, beat in two or three pieces of the chilled butter, one cube at a time. Return the saucepan to low heat and continue beating in the butter one piece at a time; the sauce will thicken considerably, becoming pale yellow in color. When all the butter has been added, immediately remove the saucepan from the heat. Stir in the tarragon and capers. Taste the beurre blanc and adjust the seasonings, adding more salt and pepper as desired.

5. Spoon the sauce generously over the fish and serve immediately.

5

PORK, LAMB, VEAL, AND BEEF
Les Viandes

Veal Stew with Mushrooms

Blanquette de veau

Serves 4–6

Blanquette de veau is an extraordinarily simple stew of veal and mushrooms, and yet I can't think of a single dish more universally adored in France. When French people rave about les cocottes de Mémé (Granny's cooking), they're probably talking about this dish. If you want to impress a French person, make them blanquette de veau. If you want to express your gratitude, make them blanquette de veau. If you want to sleep with someone . . . well—you know what to do. This dish is almost always served with rice—I prefer basmati—to soak up every last drop of sauce, of course.

---

2 pounds (1 kg) veal stew meat, trimmed into 2-inch (5-cm) pieces

1 cup (250 ml) low-sodium chicken stock

1 carrot, chopped

1 onion, studded with 1 clove

2 celery stalks chopped

½ teaspoon dried thyme

1 bay leaf

4 sprigs fresh flat-leaf parsley, including stems

Fine salt and freshly ground black pepper

3 tablespoons (45 grams) unsalted butter

2 tablespoons all-purpose flour

1. Place the veal in the pressure cooker and cover with the stock. Add the carrot, onion, celery, thyme, bay leaf, and parsley. Season lightly with salt and pepper. Cook on high pressure for 15 minutes.

2. When the veal has finished cooking, manually release the steam. Transfer the meat to a bowl. Strain the cooking liquid through a fine-mesh sieve set over a bowl, discarding the solids; set the cooking liquid aside. Wash the inner pot of the pressure cooker.

3. Using the Sauté function, melt the butter in the pressure cooker. Add the flour and cook, stirring, for 1 minute. While whisking, add the cooking liquid. Bring to a simmer and cook, whisking frequently, until the liquid has thickened, about 5 minutes. Add the mushrooms and simmer until tender, about 5 minutes, lowering the heat if the liquid simmers too rapidly. Taste the sauce and adjust the seasoning, adding more salt and pepper and/or drops of lemon juice as desired.

4. Return the meat to the pot, along with any juices from the plate. Turn off the Sauté function.

½ pound (250 grams)
   button mushrooms,
   stemmed and quartered
Fresh lemon juice (optional)
2 egg yolks
¼ cup (60 ml) sour cream
   or crème fraîche
Cooked rice, for serving

5. In a medium bowl, whisk together the egg yolks and sour cream until well combined. Remove 1 cup of the hot liquid from the pot and, while whisking, beat it into the egg yolk mixture a spoonful or two at a time to temper the egg yolks. Pour the egg yolk mixture back into the pot with the rest of the stew and use the low setting of the Sauté function to warm the stew, stirring gently—it should thicken slightly, but not come to a simmer; turn off the heat if necessary. Taste and adjust the seasonings, adding more salt and pepper as desired.

6. Serve the stew accompanied by rice.

Beef Braised in Red Wine

Bœuf bourguignon

Serves 4–6

The great classic of French country cuisine, boeuf bourguignon—made in about an hour! The magic of the pressure cooker turns the meat speedily fork-tender so that it almost melts into the rich sauce. For the wine, I suggest an inexpensive (don't spend more than $10), medium-bodied red like Beaujolais-Villages. I use frozen pearl onions to save time on peeling. If you'd like to further simplify this recipe, skip the overnight marinade—and you can also omit the mushrooms and pearl onions. Serve with boiled new potatoes, buttered broad noodles, Celery Root puree as pictured, left (page 132), or Cauliflower Gratin (134).

---

1 cup (250 ml) red wine, such as Beaujolais-Villages

2 garlic cloves, smashed

1 medium yellow onion, halved

½ teaspoon dried thyme

1 bay leaf

½ teaspoon fine salt, plus more as needed

Freshly ground black pepper

2 pounds (1 kg) beef chuck, cut into 2-inch (5-cm) cubes

1 tablespoon olive or vegetable oil, plus more as needed

3 ounces bacon (90 grams / about 3 slices), cut into ¼-inch (1.25-cm) slivers

1. In a large bowl, combine the wine, garlic, onion, thyme, bay leaf, salt, and some pepper until well mixed. Add the beef and stir to coat completely. Cover and marinate in the refrigerator overnight.

2. The next day, drain the beef, reserving the marinade, garlic cloves, and onion; discard the bay leaf. Set the marinade aside. Carefully dry the beef with paper towels and set aside on a plate. Coarsely chop the garlic cloves and onion from the marinade and set aside in a separate bowl.

3. Using the Sauté function, heat the olive oil in the pressure cooker. Add the bacon and cook until lightly browned, about 2 minutes. Transfer to a paper towel–lined plate.

4. Working in batches, add the beef cubes to the rendered bacon fat in the pressure cooker, arranging them in a single layer, and brown each side well, raising the heat if necessary to sear them, 7 to 8 minutes. Add more olive oil to the pot as needed to keep the meat from sticking. As you finish each batch, transfer the meat to a plate.

(continued)

Beef Braised in Red Wine, continued

OPTIONAL VEGETABLE
GARNISHES

2 tablespoons (30 grams)
unsalted butter

½ pound (250 grams)
button mushrooms, left
whole if small, quartered
if larger

1 cup (160 grams) frozen
pearl onions

FOR THE BEURRE MANIÉ

1 tablespoon (15 grams)
unsalted butter

1 tablespoon all-purpose
flour

Boiled new potatoes,
buttered broad noodles,
Celery Root Puree (page
132), or Cauliflower Gra-
tin (page 134), for serving

5. Reduce the heat of the Sauté function and add the reserved garlic and onion from the marinade. Cook until softened, about 2 minutes. Turn off the Sauté function. Add the reserved marinade and scrape up the browned bits from the bottom of the pot with a wooden spoon. Return the bacon and beef, along with any juices from the place, to the liquid. Cook on high pressure for 25 minutes.

6. While the beef cooks, if desired, cook the vegetable garnishes: In a large skillet, melt 1 tablespoon (15 grams) of the butter over medium-high heat. When the foam has started to subside, add the mushrooms and cook, shaking the pan frequently, until tender and lightly browned. Transfer to a bowl.

7. Melt the remaining 1 tablespoon (15 grams) butter in the skillet over medium heat and add the frozen pearl onions. Stir to combine, cover, reduce the heat to medium-low, and cook until tender, 10 to 12 minutes.

8. Prepare the beurre manié: In a small bowl, mash the flour into the butter until it forms a smooth paste.

9. When the beef has finished cooking, manually release the steam. Use a slotted spoon to transfer the beef to a plate. Strain the braising liquid through a fine-mesh sieve into a bowl, pressing on the solids to extract as much liquid as possible. Return the liquid to the pressure cooker and discard the solids.

10. Using the Sauté function, bring the liquid to a simmer. With a wire whisk, beat in the beurre manié until the sauce becomes glossy and coats the back of a spoon. Taste and adjust the seasonings, adding more salt and pepper as desired.

11. Return the beef along with any juices from the plate, the mushrooms, and pearl onions to the pressure cooker, stirring them gently into the sauce, and use a low setting of the Sauté function to gently heat them through.

12. Serve the boeuf bourguignon with boiled new potatoes, buttered broad noodles, celery root puree, or cauliflower gratin.

Note: If you don't have time to marinate the beef, proceed directly to step 3. In step 5, add the chopped onion and garlic, wine, thyme, bay leaf, salt, and pepper to taste.

Beef Braised in Beer with Spice Cookies

Carbonade

Serves 4–6

Carbonade—a hearty stew that combines beef, beer, and spice cake or cookies—is a classic Belgian recipe that's also claimed by the Picardie (nicknamed the "Ch'ti") region in northeastern France. Pain d'épices, or spice cake, is traditionally added to soften the faint bitter note of the dark ale braising liquid—but in the States you can use gingersnap or Dutch speculaas cookies, which are easier to find. Spread with a thin layer of mustard, the cookies melt into the cooking liquid, turning the sauce glossy, thick, and subtly sweet.

---

1 tablespoon olive or vegetable oil, plus more as needed

3 ounces bacon (90 grams / about 3 slices), cut into ¼-inch (1.25-cm) slivers

2 pounds (1 kg) beef chuck, cut into 2-inch (5-cm) cubes

1 medium yellow onion, diced

1 cup (250 ml) dark ale

½ teaspoon dried thyme

¼ teaspoon ground allspice

1 bay leaf

1 tablespoon honey

Fine salt and freshly ground black pepper

Dijon mustard

1. Using the Sauté function, heat the olive oil in the pressure cooker. Add the bacon and cook until lightly browned, about 2 minutes. Transfer to a paper towel–lined plate.

2. Dry the beef cubes with paper towels. Working in batches, add them to the rendered bacon fat in the pressure cooker, arranging them in a single layer, and brown each side well, 7 to 8 minutes. Add more olive oil to the pot as needed to keep the meat from sticking. As you finish each batch, transfer the meat to a plate.

3. When you've browned all the beef, add the onion to the pot and stir until softened, about 2 minutes. Turn off the Sauté function. Add the ale and stir, scraping up any browned bits from the bottom of the pot with a wooden spoon. Stir in the thyme, allspice, bay leaf, and honey.

4. Return the bacon and beef, along with any juices from the plate, to the liquid. Season lightly with salt and pepper and stir to combine. Cook on high pressure for 25 minutes.

(continued)

6 gingersnap or speculaas
  cookies (about 2 ounces
  / 50 grams), or about 2
  ounces (50 grams) *pain
  d'épices*, thinly sliced

5. Manually release the steam. Transfer the beef to a plate, leaving the liquid in the pot. Discard the bay leaf. Using the Sauté function, bring the cooking liquid to a simmer.

6. Spread a thin layer of mustard over each spice cookie. Place the cookies in the cooking liquid and break them up with a wooden spoon as they soften and dissolve in the liquid. When they've mostly dissolved, beat the sauce with a wire whisk to fully incorporate. Cook the sauce, stirring continuously, until it thickens and becomes glossy. Taste and adjust the seasonings, adding more salt and pepper as desired.

7. Return the beef to the sauce along with any juices from the plate, and gently reheat before serving.

Provençal Beef Stew

Daube provençale

Serves 4–6

Daube is the classic braised dish of southern France, and almost any tough cut of meat can be prepared this way, from lamb to pheasant. The daube is similar to boeuf bourguignon, with its red wine cooking liquid, but it's more casual, adding a pinch of this or that. In this spirit, I've made this recipe quick and informal, skipping the tedious and messy task of browning the meat. Along with the fennel, a handful of black olives and a final dusting of orange zest add a particularly Provençal flavor.

1 tablespoon olive oil

3 ounces bacon (90 grams / about 3 slices), cut crosswise into ½-inch (1.5-cm) lardons

1 medium onion, diced

1 medium fennel bulb, trimmed and diced

2 garlic cloves, thinly sliced

1 cup (250 ml) red wine

2 pounds (1 kg) beef chuck, cut into 2-inch (5-cm) cubes

2 carrots, cut into ½-inch (1.25-cm) rounds

¼ teaspoon dried thyme

¼ teaspoon dried oregano

1 bay leaf

½ teaspoon fennel seeds

1. Using the Sauté function, heat the olive oil in the pressure cooker. Add the bacon and cook until lightly browned, about 2 minutes. Transfer to a paper towel–lined plate.

2. Add the onion and fennel to the pot and cook until softened, about 2 minutes. Add the garlic and cook until fragrant, about 30 seconds. Turn off the Sauté function. Add the wine and stir, scraping up any browned bits from the bottom of the pot with a wooden spoon. Add the beef, carrots, thyme, oregano, bay leaf, and fennel seeds. Season lightly with salt and pepper and stir to combine. Cook on high pressure for 25 minutes.

3. While the beef cooks, in a small bowl, mash the flour into the butter until it forms a smooth paste (this is the beurre manié).

4. When the beef has finished cooking, manually release the pressure. Transfer the beef to a plate, leaving the liquid in the pot, and add the olives to the liquid. Discard the bay leaf.

(continued)

Fine salt and freshly ground
   black pepper
1 tablespoon all-purpose
   flour
1 tablespoon (15 grams)
   unsalted butter
¼ cup (40 grams) pitted
   oil-cured black olives
Zest of 1 orange

5. Using the Sauté function, bring the cooking liquid to a simmer. With a wire whisk, beat in the beurre manié until the sauce becomes glossy and coats the back of a spoon. Taste and adjust the seasonings, adding more salt and pepper as desired. Return beef to the sauce along with any juices from the plate, and gently warm everything through.

6. Serve sprinkled with the orange zest.

Short Rib Shepherd's Pie

Hachis Parmentier

Born in the eighteenth century, French pharmacist and agronomist Antoine-Augustin Parmentier is known as the man who popularized the potato in France. Today he's celebrated with a Paris métro station, and with this potato-topped meat pie, found commonly on bistro menus. This rendition uses short ribs, which are luscious and rich. They also produce a lot of fat, so I recommend skimming the cooking liquid before thickening it, even if that seems a bit fussy.

---

2 tablespoons olive or vegetable oil, plus more as needed

3 to 4 pounds (1½ to 2 kg) beef chuck short ribs, trimmed of excess fat

2 carrots, diced

1 onion, diced

1 celery stalk, diced

1 cup (250 ml) red wine

1 tablespoon tomato paste

½ teaspoon dried thyme

1 bay leaf

1 teaspoon ground coriander

Fine salt and freshly ground black pepper

1 tablespoon all-purpose flour

2 pounds (1 kg) potatoes, preferably Yukon Gold, peeled and quartered

1. Using the Sauté function, heat the olive oil in the pressure cooker. Working in batches, add the short ribs to the pot and brown well on each side. Add more olive oil to the pot as needed to keep the meat from sticking. As you finish each batch, transfer the ribs to a plate.

2. When all the ribs have been browned, add the carrots, onion, and celery to the pot and cook until softened. Turn off the Sauté function. Add the wine and stir, scraping up any browned bits from the bottom of the pot with a wooden spoon. Return the browned short ribs to the pot along with any juices from the plate, and add the tomato paste, thyme, bay leaf, and coriander. Season lightly with salt and pepper and stir to combine. Cook on high pressure for 55 minutes.

3. Manually release the pressure. Remove the short ribs, set them aside on a plate, and allow them to cool slightly. Pour the vegetables and braising liquid into a medium bowl or large measuring cup and use a spoon to skim off the fat at the top (there will be a lot), reserving 1 tablespoon. Discard the bay leaf. In a small bowl, whisk together the reserved 1 tablespoon fat and the flour to form a thickening agent.

(continued)

¼ cup (60 ml) whole milk, warmed

4 tablespoons (½ stick / 60 grams) unsalted butter

1 egg yolk

Pinch of grated nutmeg

4. Wash the inner pot of the pressure cooker. Place the steaming rack inside and add 1 cup (250 ml) water. Arrange the potatoes on the rack. Cook on high pressure for 5 minutes.

5. While the potatoes are cooking, pull the bones from the ribs. Shred the meat into bite-size pieces, discarding any excess gristle.

6. Preheat the oven to 400°F (200°C).

7. Pour the vegetables and braising liquid into a medium saucepan and bring to a simmer over medium heat. Cook until the liquid has reduced by half, about 10 minutes. Add the thickening agent and stir until the sauce becomes glossy. Taste and add more salt and pepper if desired. Fold the shredded meat into the sauce.

8. When the potatoes have finished cooking, manually release the steam. Drain the potatoes, remove the steaming rack, and pour any water out of the pot. Return the potatoes to the pot. Add the milk, butter, and egg yolk and use a potato masher to crush the potatoes smooth. Taste and season with the nutmeg and more salt and pepper as desired.

9. Transfer the short rib mixture to a 9 x 13-inch (23 x 33-cm) baking dish, or divide it among four to six individual dishes. Cover the top(s) evenly with the potatoes. Bake until the sauce bubbles and the potatoes turn golden, 35 to 40 minutes.

Whole Stuffed Cabbage

Chou farci

Serves 6–8

For years, I admired photos of whole stuffed cabbages, but the intricately layered creations of meat and cabbage always seemed too complex to attempt myself. It turns out, however, the preparation is not so difficult, especially if you combine Jacques Pépin's genius cabbage-stuffing technique—as he describes in Julia and Jacques Cooking at Home*—with the pressure cooker, which reduces the cooking time by half.*

In this recipe, a whole cabbage is taken apart leaf by leaf and then reassembled with layers of ground meat and rice. I was inspired by Jacques Pépin's version, but I invented my own stuffing, perfuming it with winter herbs. The accompanying light tomato sauce is the perfect foil against the rich, savory cabbage.

---

1 medium head savoy cabbage

2 tablespoons olive or vegetable oil

1 onion, chopped

1 ½ cups (375 ml) chicken stock

1 pound (500 grams) ground beef

2 cups (240 grams) cooked white rice

2 garlic cloves, minced

2 teaspoons minced fresh rosemary, plus more as desired

2 teaspoons minced fresh sage, plus more as desired

2 large eggs

1. Prepare the cabbage by separating 20 leaves from the head, working inward from the larger leaves to the smaller ones. (To separate the leaves, run a thin stream of cold tap water where the edge of the leaf meets the head, allowing the water to gently tease away the leaf.) Use a sharp knife to cut the base of the leaf and remove it from the core. When you've removed 20 leaves, halve the cabbage heart, remove the tough core, and finely chop the leaves; set them aside to use in the stuffing.

2. Place the steaming rack in the pressure cooker and add 1 cup (250 ml) water. Arrange half the cabbage leaves on the rack. (You will need to steam them in two batches.) Cook on high pressure for 0 minutes (see page xxii), bringing the cooker to pressure and then immediately releasing the steam. Manually release the steam, set the cabbage leaves aside on a plate, and repeat with the second batch of leaves.

3. Using kitchen shears, snip away 1 to 2 inches (2.5 to 5 cm) of the tough central rib from the base of each leaf. Set the leaves aside on a plate.

4. In a sauté pan, heat the olive oil over medium heat. Add the chopped cabbage

(continued)

2 teaspoons fine salt, plus
more as desired

½ teaspoon freshly ground
black pepper, plus more
as desired

1 cup (250 ml) canned
crushed tomatoes

heart and the onion and cook until wilted. Season lightly with salt and pepper, add ½ cup (125 ml) of the stock, cover, and cook until most of the liquid has evaporated and the vegetables are soft, about 10 minutes. Remove from the heat and let cool to lukewarm.

5. In a large bowl, combine the ground beef, rice, garlic, rosemary, sage, eggs, salt, pepper, and the cooled onion-cabbage mixture. Mix thoroughly with your hands.

(If you'd like to check the seasoning, fry a spoonful of the stuffing in a small skillet; taste it and add more salt, pepper, rosemary, and/or sage as desired.)

6. To form the stuffed cabbage, lay an 18-inch (45-cm) square of aluminum foil on the counter. Arrange 5 of the largest cabbage leaves in a rough circle, 12 to 14 inches (30 to 35 cm) in diameter, overlapping the leaves and with the notched base of each leaf on the exterior of the circle. Spread about a third of the stuffing in the center of the circle of leaves, leaving a 2- to 3-inch (5- to 7.5-cm) border.

7. Cover the stuffing with a layer of 4 or 5 more leaves, making the second circle slightly smaller than the first. Spread another third of the stuffing on top, leaving a border of 2 to 3 inches. Repeat with a third layer of leaves, making the circle slightly smaller than the second one, and top with the remaining stuffing. Finally, cover the stuffing with a layer of the smallest leaves, forming the smallest circle.

8. Lift the four corners of the foil and gather them together so that the larger leaves (those in the bottommost layer) cover the inner leaves and stuffing. Pat the foil package into a round cabbage shape, leaving a small opening—a vent hole—at the top.

9. Place the steaming rack in the pressure cooker and add the remaining 1 cup (250 ml) stock. Flip the stuffed cabbage upside down so the vent hole is at the bottom and place it on the steaming rack. Cook on high pressure for 60 minutes.

10. Allow the steam to release naturally. Carefully lift out the steaming rack with stuffed cabbage on top and set it aside on a cutting board or platter, leaving the liquid in the pot. Using the Sauté function, bring the cooking liquid to a simmer and add the crushed tomatoes, stirring to combine. Simmer briskly until the sauce thickens slightly, about 5 minutes. Taste and add salt and pepper as desired.

11. Unwrap the foil from the cabbage, set it on a serving plate, and slice it into wedges. Serve with the sauce on the side.

White Beans with Pork and Duck

Cassoulet

Serves 4–6

According to legend, the town of Castelnaudary, in the Languedoc-Roussillon region of France, is the birthplace of cassoulet, invented in the fourteenth century. And, indeed, the Castelnaudarians take it very seriously. Today, a local society, La Grande Confrérie du Cassoulet de Castelnaudary, protects the integrity of the dish, claiming that it needs to be cooked for hours, cooled, and cooked again—and then again after that! I am sure that the Grande Confrérie would not support the idea of a quick pressure cooker cassoulet—but I challenge anyone to tell the difference. Note that though the crisped bread crumb topping is not at all traditional, it is delicious— but if you're pressed for time (or a purist) you can skip it.

1 pound (500 grams) unsoaked dried great northern beans, rinsed and sorted for debris

2 garlic cloves, crushed

¼ pound (125 grams) fresh pork skin, cut into 2-inch (5-cm) squares (optional)

2 duck confit thighs

½ pound (250 grams) garlic sausage, cut into large chunks

¼ pound (125 grams) pork shoulder, cut into large chunks

½ teaspoon grated nutmeg

2 tablespoons tomato paste

Fine salt and freshly ground black pepper

1. Put the dried beans in a large bowl and add cold water to cover. Set aside to soak overnight. The next day, drain the beans and place them in the pressure cooker. Add the garlic, pork skin (if using), and 2 quarts (2 L) water. Cook on high pressure for 5 minutes. (Alternatively, if you don't have time to soak the beans, cook with the garlic, pork, and water, on high pressure for 15 minutes.)

2. While the beans are cooking, in a large sauté pan, brown the duck thighs over medium-low heat until golden on all sides, then transfer them to a large plate. Add the sausage and chunks of pork to the fat remaining in the pan and brown them on all sides. Transfer to the plate.

3. When the beans have finished cooking, manually release the steam. Using a ladle, remove 5 cups of the bean cooking liquid from the pot and set aside.

4. Stir the nutmeg, tomato paste, 1 teaspoon salt, and pepper to taste into the beans. Add the browned duck thighs, sausage, and pork shoulder. Cook on high pressure for 20 minutes.

(continued)

OPTIONAL BREAD CRUMB
TOPPING

1 cup (50 grams) dried or
    fresh bread crumbs

3 tablespoons olive oil

5. Allow the pressure to release naturally for 10 minutes, then manually release the steam. Taste the cassoulet and adjust the seasonings, adding more salt and pepper as desired. At this point, the cassoulet will appear quite liquid, but it will thicken as it rests. If you can wait, allow it to rest for about 20 minutes before serving. (The cassoulet will thicken further—and tastes even better—after it has cooled completely, been refrigerated overnight, and then reheated.)

6. If you are making the bread crumb topping, two hours before serving, preheat the oven to 350°F (175°C).

7. In a large bowl, mix the bread crumbs with the olive oil until thoroughly combined. Transfer the cassoulet to a wide 8-quart (8-L) braising vessel. If the cassoulet is too thick, add a bit of stock or water to loosen it. Spread the bread crumbs in an even layer over the top and bake for 90 minutes, until the cassoulet is bubbling slightly and heated through and the bread crumbs are golden brown. If the bread crumbs are still too pale, turn the oven to broil and brown the top, watching carefully so they don't burn.

Veal Stew with Tomatoes and Mushrooms

Veau Marengo

Serves 4

Reportedly a favorite of Napoléon Bonaparte, this savory dish of veal (or chicken), tomatoes, garlic, and white wine was allegedly created after the Battle of Marengo in 1800. It's often found on school lunch menus as the plat du jour, and as a result evokes an air of nostalgia for many French people.

2 tablespoons olive or vegetable oil

2 pounds (1 kg) veal stew meat, cut into 2-inch (5-cm) cubes

2 onions, chopped

1 tablespoon all-purpose flour

¼ cup (60 ml) white wine

1 pound (500 grams) tomatoes, chopped

1 garlic clove, crushed

½ teaspoon dried thyme

1 bay leaf

Fine salt and freshly ground black pepper

1 tablespoon (15 grams) unsalted butter

½ pound (250 grams) brown button mushrooms, sliced

Chopped fresh flat-leaf parsley, for garnish

1. Using the Sauté function, heat the olive oil in the pressure cooker. Pat the veal dry with paper towels. Working in batches, add the veal cubes, arranging them in a single layer, and brown each side well, 7 to 8 minutes. Add more olive oil to the pot as needed to keep the meat from sticking. As you finish each batch, transfer the meat to a plate.

2. Add the onions to the pot and cook until softened. Sprinkle over the flour and stir to combine. Turn off the Sauté function. Add the wine and stir, scraping up any browned bits from the bottom of the pot with a wooden spoon. Add the tomatoes, garlic, thyme, and bay leaf. Season lightly with salt and pepper. Cook on high pressure for 15 minutes.

3. While the veal is cooking, in a medium skillet, melt the butter over medium-high heat until foamy. When the foam has started to subside, add the mushrooms and cook, shaking the pan frequently, until tender and lightly browned. Season lightly with salt and pepper. Transfer to a bowl.

4. When the veal has finished cooking, allow the pressure to release naturally. Transfer the meat to a plate, leaving the liquid in the pot. Discard the bay leaf. Using the Sauté function, bring the braising liquid to a rapid bowl and cook until slightly thickened, about 5 minutes. Taste, adding more salt and pepper as desired.

5. Return the veal to the sauce along with the mushrooms, and gently heat through. Garnish with parsley, if desired, and serve.

Braised Pork with Apples

Porc à la normande

Serves 4–6

This recipe uses all these ingredients for a simple, rich, and wintry stew that comes quickly together with the help of the pressure cooker.

1 tablespoon olive or vegetable oil, plus more as needed

3 slices bacon, cut cross-wise into ½-inch (1.5-cm) lardons

2 pounds (1 kg) pork shoulder, cut into 2-inch (5-cm) cubes

1 medium onion, diced

1 celery stalk, diced

2 carrots, cut into ½-inch (1.25-cm) rounds

1 cup (250 ml) dry hard cider

½ teaspoon dried thyme

Fine salt and freshly ground black pepper

1 firm cooking apple, such as Honeycrisp or Fuji, peeled, cored, and cut into 1-inch (2.5-cm) chunks

1 tablespoon whole-grain Dijon mustard

3 tablespoons crème fraîche or sour cream

1. Using the Sauté function, heat the olive oil in the pressure cooker. Add the bacon and cook until lightly browned, about 2 minutes. Transfer to a paper towel–lined plate.

2. Dry the pork cubes with paper towels. Working in batches, add them to the rendered bacon fat in the pressure cooker, arranging them in a single layer, and brown each side well, 7 to 8 minutes. Add more olive oil to the pot as needed to keep the meat from sticking. As you finish each batch, transfer the meat to a plate.

3. Add the onion, celery, and carrots to the pot and cook until softened slightly, about 2 minutes. Turn off the Sauté function. Add the hard cider and stir, scraping up any browned bits from the bottom of the pot with a wooden spoon.

4. Return the bacon and pork to the pot and add the thyme. Season lightly with salt and pepper and stir to combine. Cook on high pressure for 20 minutes.

5. Manually release the steam. Transfer the pork to a plate, leaving the liquid in the pot. Using the Sauté function, bring the cooking liquid to a simmer. Add the apple and cook until tender, about 10 minutes. Turn off the Sauté function.

6. With a wire whisk, beat the mustard and crème fraîche into the sauce. Taste and adjust the seasonings, adding more salt and pepper if necessary. Return the pork to the sauce, along with any juices from the plate, and use the Sauté function to gently heat everything through before serving.

Lamb Tagine with Prunes

Tajine d'agneau aux pruneaux

Serves 4

A tagine takes its name from a North African earthenware vessel featuring a flat bottom and conical lid. I first tried this dish of tender braised lamb and succulent prunes in a Moroccan restaurant in Paris, and found the contrast of honey, spices, fruit, and meat a heady combination. Serve this dish with couscous to soak up the sauce, and accompany it with little dishes of chickpeas, raisins, and harissa, like they do in Paris.

---

2 tablespoons olive oil
Pinch of saffron
1 teaspoon ground cumin
1 teaspoon sweet paprika
1 teaspoon fine salt, plus
  more as desired
Freshly ground black
  pepper
2 pounds (1 kg) lamb
  shoulder, trimmed of fat
  and cut into 2-inch
  (5-cm) pieces
1 onion, chopped
3 garlic cloves, minced
8 ounces (250 grams)
  dried pitted prunes
1 tablespoon honey, plus
  more as desired
1 teaspoon ground
  cinnamon, plus more
  as desired

1. In a large bowl, stir together the olive oil, saffron, cumin, paprika, salt, and some pepper. Add the lamb and stir to coat with the marinade. Marinate in the refrigerator for at least 30 minutes or up to overnight.

2. Using the Sauté function, heat the pressure cooker. Working in batches, add the lamb cubes, arranging them in a single layer, and brown each side well, 7 to 8 minutes. As you finish each batch, transfer the meat to a plate.

3. Add the onion and garlic to the pressure cooker and cook until softened slightly, about 2 minutes. Turn off the Sauté function. Add 1 cup (250 ml) water, scraping up any browned bits from the bottom of the pot with a wooden spoon. Return the lamb cubes to the pot and stir to combine. Cook on high pressure for 15 minutes.

4. While the lamb is cooking, in a small saucepan, combine the prunes, honey, cinnamon, and ½ cup (125 ml) water. Bring to a simmer over medium-low heat and cook until the prunes are very soft and most of the liquid has been absorbed, about 15 minutes. Remove from the heat.

5. When the lamb has finished cooking, manually release the steam. Transfer the meat to a plate. Add the prunes and their cooking liquid to the pressure cooker.

Toasted sesame seeds, for garnish (optional)

Cooked couscous, for serving

Using the Sauté function, simmer the liquid until it thickens slightly, 2 to 4 minutes. Taste the sauce and adjust the seasonings, adding more salt, pepper, honey, and/or cinnamon as desired.

6. Return the lamb and any juices from the plate to the pressure cooker and gently heat through. Garnish with toasted sesame seeds, if desired, and serve with couscous.

Stuffed Tomatoes and Rice

Tomates farcies accompagnées de riz

Serves 4

Tomates farcies, the juicy bright globes stuffed with ground meat and fresh herbs, are a favorite summer dish in Provence. This recipe is the epitome of French thrift, repurposing the juice and pulp from the hollowed-out tomatoes to prepare the accompanying rice. And by using the steaming rack of the pressure cooker, you can cook both the stuffed tomatoes and the rice together in only five minutes, making this an ingenious one-pot meal.

---

8 medium tomatoes, about 5 ounces (140 grams) each

2 slices stale bread (about 2 ounces / 55 grams)

½ cup (125 ml) milk

2 tablespoons (30 grams) unsalted butter

½ cup (90 grams) finely chopped onion

½ pound (250 grams) ground beef, pork, or veal (or any combination)

3 garlic cloves, minced

½ cup (55 grams) grated hard cheese, like Gruyère, Comté, or Parmesan

2 large eggs

½ teaspoon dried thyme

1. Slice off the top quarter of each tomato, reserving the lids. With a paring knife, core the tomatoes and use a small spoon to scoop out the interior, reserving the juice and pulp.

2. Soak the bread in the milk.

3. In a sauté pan, melt 1 tablespoon (15 grams) of the butter over medium heat. Add the onion and cook until softened, about 3 minutes. Let cool slightly.

4. Transfer the onion to a large bowl and add the ground meat, garlic, cheese, and eggs. Drain the bread and add it to the bowl. Add the thyme, oregano, mint (if using), 2 teaspoons salt, and pepper to taste. Combine thoroughly, using your hands if necessary.

5. Season each tomato cavity with a pinch each of salt and pepper. Stuff the tomatoes with the meat mixture, heaping it over the top. Replace the lid of each tomato.

6. Using the Sauté function, melt the remaining 1 tablespoon (15 grams) butter in the pressure cooker. Put the rice in a fine-mesh sieve and rinse it under cold water, then add it to the pressure cooker, stirring to coat the grains with the butter. Turn off the Sauté function. Measure the reserved tomato juice and pulp, adding more

½ teaspoon dried oregano

2 tablespoons chopped
fresh mint or parsley,
plus more as desired
(optional)

Fine salt and freshly ground
black pepper

1 cup (200 grams) long-
grained rice, such as
basmati

water (if necessary) to make 1½ cups liquid. Stir this mixture into the rice, along with 1 teaspoon salt.

7. Place the steaming rack in the pressure cooker on top of the rice, making sure that all four legs touch the bottom. Arrange the stuffed tomatoes upright on the steaming rack. Cook on high pressure for 5 minutes.

8. Allow the pressure to release naturally. Garnish the stuffed tomatoes with chopped herbs, if desired, and serve accompanied by the rice.

Braised Beef Pot Roast

Boeuf à la mode

Serves 6–8

Pot roast is a simple, old-fashioned country dish, eaten often in French homes and rarely seen in restaurants. Thanks to the pressure cooker, this homey dish is even easier and faster to prepare. À la mode means literally "in the style of"—but, as my friend Didier instructed me, most people usually shorten the name of this dish, calling it simply boeuf mode. Note that a square of pork rind adds body and richness to the sauce, but it is optional.

---

2 cups (500 ml) red wine, such as Beaujolais-Villages

1 onion, chopped

1 carrot, chopped

1 celery stalk, chopped

2 garlic cloves, crushed

1 teaspoon dried thyme

1 bay leaf

1 teaspoon fine salt, plus more as desired

Freshly ground black pepper

1 (3- to 4-pound / 1.5- to 2-kg) beef rump or chuck roast, trimmed and tied

2 tablespoons olive or vegetable oil

4 ounces (125 grams) fresh pork rind (optional)

2 tablespoons all-purpose flour

1. In a large bowl, combine the wine, onion, carrot, celery, garlic, thyme, bay leaf, salt, and some pepper. Add the beef and stir to coat with the marinade. Cover and marinate in the refrigerator for at least 1 hour or up to overnight.

2. Drain the beef, reserving the vegetables and marinade.

3. Dry the beef with paper towels. Using the Sauté function, heat the olive oil in the pressure cooker. Add the beef and brown it on all sides, 3 to 4 minutes per side. Transfer the beef to a large plate.

4. Return the vegetables to the pot and cook until softened, about 3 minutes. Add the reserved marinade and stir, scraping up any browned bits from the bottom of the pot with a wooden spoon. Return the beef to the pot, nestling it into the braising liquid. Add the pork skin (if using). Cook on high pressure for 60 minutes.

5. While the beef is cooking, in a small bowl, mash the flour into the butter until it forms a smooth paste (this is the beurre manié).

6. When the beef has finished cooking, manually release the steam. Transfer the beef to a platter, leaving the liquid in the pot. Discard the bay leaf. Cut away the trussing strings and tent the meat with a piece of aluminum foil to keep it warm.

2 tablespoons (30 grams)
unsalted butter
½ teaspoon sugar, plus
more as desired

7. Skim the fat from the braising liquid. Using the Sauté function, bring the liquid to a rapid bowl and cook until it has reduced by about a third.

8. Using a whisk, beat in the beurre manié so that the sauce thickens and becomes glossy. Stir in the sugar and taste the sauce, adding sugar and more salt, and pepper as desired.

9. Carve the meat and serve, passing the sauce at the table.

6

VEGETABLES
Les Legumes

Provençal White Beans

Haricots blancs à la provençale

Serves 6

The word Provence *evokes sun, summer heat, and all the glorious produce of the South of France. I spent six wonderful vacations with my husband in a hillside village in the Luberon, washing down idleness with sips of chilled rosé. Alas, when the house we used to rent was sold, we somehow never found our way back. But I still think of Provence often—at least once a week—imagining the sharp light and soft breezes. And when the nostalgia hits, I make these beans, rich with fine olive oil and perfumed with the native herbs of this region that I love so much.*

---

1 pound (500 grams) unsoaked dried cannellini beans, rinsed and sorted for debris

3 tablespoons extra-virgin olive oil

1 onion, diced

3 celery stalks, with leaves, diced

2 garlic cloves, minced

1 (28-ounce / 794-gram) can crushed tomatoes

½ teaspoon dried thyme

1 small sprig fresh rosemary, or ½ teaspoon dried

½ teaspoon dried oregano

1½ teaspoons fine salt

½ teaspoon freshly ground black pepper

extra-virgin olive oil

1. Put the beans in a bowl and add cold water to cover by 3 inches (7.5 cm). Set aside to soak overnight.

2. The next day, using the Sauté function, heat the olive oil in the pressure cooker. Add the onion and celery and cook until soft, about 6 minutes. Add the garlic and cook for 30 seconds.

3. Add the crushed tomatoes and simmer briskly, stirring frequently, until the sauce thickens, about 3 minutes. (This is messy and the tomatoes will spatter.)

4. Drain the beans and add them to the tomato sauce, along with the thyme, rosemary, oregano, salt, pepper, and 3 cups (750 ml) water, stirring to combine. Cook on high pressure for 20 minutes.

5. Manually release the steam. Taste the beans and adjust the seasonings, adding more salt and pepper as desired. Serve drizzled with extra-virgin olive oil.

Carrots with Cream

Carottes à la crème

Serves 4

Carrots are a staple of the long, dark, French winters, commonly found in soups or stews, and also enjoyed as a colorful side dish, as in this simple preparation. Though I am not generally a fan of cooked carrots, I love this recipe, which becomes decadent with only a couple spoonfuls of cream.

1½ teaspoons vegetable or olive oil

1 small onion, diced

1½ pounds (750 grams) carrots, cut into ¼-inch-thick (6-mm) rounds

1 whole clove

Fine salt and freshly ground black pepper

2 tablespoons sour cream or crème fraîche

2 tablespoons minced fresh parsley, chives, and/or dill (optional)

1. Using the Sauté function, heat the oil in the pressure cooker. Add the onion and cook until softened but not browned. Turn off the Sauté function.

2. Add the carrots, clove, and 1 cup (250 ml) water to the pot, season lightly with salt and pepper, and stir to combine. Cook on high pressure for 2 minutes.

3. Manually release the steam. Remove the lid and allow the carrots to rest and reabsorb some of the liquid they have released, 3 to 5 minutes.

4. Using the Sauté function, add the sour cream to the carrots and warm through, stirring gently to combine. (If there is still too much liquid, cook for 3 to 5 minutes to reduce it.) Taste and adjust the seasonings, adding more salt and pepper as desired. Gently toss the minced herbs into the carrots before serving, if desired.

Crispy Potatoes

Pommes fondantes

Serves 4–6

My French neighbor, Matthieu, told me about this dish while we were waiting for the school bus to bring our kids home. His grandmother made potatoes like these—albeit without the help of the pressure cooker, which greatly speeds up the process. The potatoes undergo a quick steam, which brings starch to their surface—when roasted, this starch turns to a crisp shell, while the interior becomes fluffy. The addition of unpeeled garlic cloves adds a delightful piquancy—Matthieu calls them ail en chaussettes—"garlic in socks."

2 pounds (1 kg) Yukon Gold potatoes
2 tablespoons olive oil
1 teaspoon fine salt
½ head garlic, cloves separated

1. Preheat the oven to 500°F (260°C). Line a baking sheet with parchment paper.

2. Peel the potatoes and slice them into irregular pieces, about 1 inch (2.5 cm) in size.

3. Place the steaming rack in the pressure cooker and add 1 cup (250 ml) water. Arrange the potatos on the rack. Cook on high pressure for 0 minutes (see page xxii), bringing the cooker to pressure and then immediately releasing the steam.

4. When the potatoes have finished cooking, manually release the steam. Transfer the potatoes to a bowl and add the olive oil and salt, stirring gently to combine. The surface of the potatoes will appear sticky and fuzzy.

5. Arrange the potatoes in a single layer on the prepared baking sheet. Roast for 20 minutes. Remove the baking sheet, turn the potatoes so they brown evenly, and scatter over the garlic cloves. Return the baking sheet to the oven and roast for 15 to 20 minutes, or until the potatoes are crisp and golden brown. Serve immediately.

Braised Peppers, Tomatoes, and Onion

Pipérade

Serves 4–6

Pipérade is a classic Basque dish of stewed peppers and tomatoes, seasoned with piment d'Espelette, the mild, round-flavored chile cultivated in the region, sun-dried, and ground into a powder. The traditional recipe uses green peppers—specifically, a variety called pipèr, which give the recipe its name—but I've found that ordinary supermarket peppers turn the dish too bitter. Instead, I use a tiny amount of green bell peppers with a generous quantity of red to balance the flavors—but feel free to use only red if you prefer a sweeter dish. If you can't find piment d'Espelette, sweet paprika is a fine substitute. Pipérade can be made in advance and refrigerated. It's traditionally served with scrambled eggs and lightly fried country ham, or tucked into an omelet. I love it with an egg cooked on top—shakshuka-style (See Note below and photo on facing page). It's also a wonderful side dish with roasted meat or fish.

---

2 tablespoons olive oil

1 medium yellow onion, diced

1 pound (500 grams) red bell peppers, sliced

4 ounces (100 grams) green bell pepper, sliced

2 garlic cloves, finely sliced

1 pound (500 grams) tomatoes, peeled and diced

½ teaspoon sugar

½ teaspoon piment *d'Espelette* or sweet paprika

Fine salt and freshly ground black pepper

4–6 large eggs, for serving

1. Using the Sauté function, heat the olive oil in the pressure cooker. Add the onion and red and green bell peppers and cook until softened, about 2 minutes. Add the garlic and cook until fragrant, about 1 minute. Turn off the Sauté function.

2. Add the tomatoes, sugar, and piment d'Espelette to the pressure cooker. Season lightly and stir to combine. Cook on high pressure for 6 minutes.

3. Manually release the steam. Using the Sauté function, bring the mixture to a simmer. Cook, stirring occasionally, until most of the liquid has evaporated, about 8 minutes. Taste and adjust the seasonings, adding salt and black pepper as desired.

Note: Pipérade is traditionally served with scrambled eggs, or as an omelet filling. It's also delicious with an egg cooked on top, shakshuka style. To prepare the latter, warm the pipérade in a skillet over low heat until bubbling gently. Using the back of a spoon, make an indentation for each egg in the mixture. Crack an egg into its indentation. Cover the skillet and cook until the whites are set and the yolks film over, 2 to 3 minutes.

Celery Root Puree

Purée de céleri-rave

Serves 4

Celery root—celeriac, or céleri-rave in French—is sometimes called a legume oublié, a quaint way to refer to root vegetables like parsnips or beets that have fallen out of fashion. It tastes like a milder version of celery, and is often eaten crunchy and raw, as in the coleslaw-like salad céleri rémoulade. When cooked, it softens into a smooth puree so silky it only needs a touch of butter. This is an alternative to mashed potatoes, and pairs well with braised dishes like boeuf bourguignon as pictured on page 92 or roasted meats.

---

1 pound (500 grams) celery root (celeriac)

½ pound (250 grams) starchy potatoes like Russet, peeled and cut into 1-inch (2.5-cm) cubes

2 garlic cloves, thinly sliced

½ teaspoon fine salt

2 tablespoons (30 grams) unsalted butter

Freshly ground black pepper

1. Using a sharp chef's knife, cut off the top and bottom ends of the celery root. Place the root on a cutting board on one of the flat sides so that it is stable. Cut away the rough peel in vertical strips, following the curved shape of the root. Remove any small or stubborn bits of skin with a vegetable peeler. Cut the celery root into 1-inch (2.5-cm) cubes.

2. Put the celery root and potato in the pressure cooker and add the garlic, salt, and ½ cup (125 ml) water. Stir to combine. Cook on high pressure for 8 minutes.

3. Manually release the steam. With an immersion blender, puree the vegetables directly in the pot until smooth. Beat in the butter with a wooden spoon. Taste and add more salt and a few turns of the pepper mill, if desired.

THE PRESSURE COOKER AS A SHORTCUT

Obviously, the pressure cooker is great for one-pot meals. But French home cooks also rely on it as a time-saver, to shorten or simplify a step in a recipe. They use it to soften cauliflower for a gratin, to steam endives for endives au jambon, or to cook tough-skinned winter squashes into silky purees. My friend Thomas cooks a big batch of potatoes on the weekends and uses them throughout the week, fried with duck fat, tucked into omelets, or thrown into salads.

Once you start considering the pressure cooker as a shortcut, the possibilities are endless!

Cauliflower Gratin

Gratin de chou-fleur

Serves 4–6

In French, the word gratin *is also a slang term for the social elite or the upper crust; but, this golden-crusted dish has universal appeal. Here the pressure cooker is used as a shortcut, speedily softening the cauliflower to the perfect texture. Emmenthal is the traditional cheese for gratins in France—indeed, it's the country's favorite grated cheese; a bag of it can be found in almost every French fridge—but I think it's too bland. Instead, I prefer a combination of Gruyère and—gasp!— cheddar, which, though not French, adds a desirable tang. The dash of cayenne pepper isn't traditional, either, but I like its sparky kick.*

2½ pounds (1 kg) cauliflower, trimmed into 1-inch (2.5-cm) florets

2 slices (70 grams) white or whole-wheat sandwich bread

3 tablespoons (45 grams) unsalted butter

1 cup (120 grams) grated Comté or Gruyère cheese

½ cup (60 grams) grated sharp cheddar cheese

3 tablespoons all-purpose flour

2 cups (500 ml) milk

Pinch of grated nutmeg

Pinch of cayenne pepper (optional)

Fine salt and freshly ground black pepper

1. Place the steaming rack in the pressure cooker and add 1 cup (250 ml) water. Place the cauliflower florets on the rack. Cook on high pressure for 0 minutes (see page xxii), bringing the cooker to pressure and then immediately releasing the steam.

2. While the cauliflower is cooking, tear the sandwich bread into large pieces and place them in a food processor. Pulse three or four times to form coarse crumbs. Transfer to a large bowl. Melt 1 tablespoon (15 grams) of the butter and stir it into the bread crumbs. Combine the grated cheeses in a bowl or measuring cup. Remove ¼ cup (30 grams) of the cheese mixture and combine it with the bread crumbs; set the remaining cheese aside.

3. When the cauliflower has finished cooking, manually release the steam. Transfer the cauliflower to a bowl.

4. Preheat the oven to 375ºF (190ºC).

5. In a medium saucepan, melt the remaining 2 tablespoons (30 grams) butter over low heat. Add the flour and cook, stirring continuously, until the mixture smells slightly toasty, about 5 minutes. Pour in the milk and whisk until the mixture begins to thicken. Boil for 1 minute, whisking continuously. Remove from the heat.

Add the remaining grated cheeses, the nutmeg, cayenne (if using), and salt and black pepper to taste. Stir well to melt the cheese and incorporate. Taste and adjust the seasonings.

6. Pour one-third of the sauce into an 11 x 7 x 2-inch (28 x 18 x 5-cm) baking dish. Arrange the cauliflower on top and evenly pour the remaining sauce over the cauliflower. Sprinkle the bread crumb mixture evenly over the top.

7. Bake for 20 to 25 minutes, or until the sauce is bubbling and the bread crumbs are golden brown.

Green Beans Braised in Tomato Sauce

Haricots verts à la provençale

Serves 4–6

These days, green beans are most often cooked just until crisp-tender, bright in color, and squeaky be-tween the teeth. But if you've never tried them braised—until meltingly soft and silky—you've been missing out. Green beans in tomato sauce is a classic Mediterranean recipe, cooked for hours, sometimes perfumed with cinnamon, as in Greece, or sprinkled with summer herbs like basil, as in Provence. The pressure cooker makes quick work of the braising, softening the beans in just a few minutes.

---

1 pound (500 grams) fresh
green beans
2 tablespoons olive oil
1 onion, diced
2 garlic cloves, thinly sliced
1 cup (250 ml) canned
whole tomatoes, lightly
crushed by hand
Fine salt and freshly ground
black pepper
¼ cup fresh basil leaves,
rolled and thinly sliced
into ribbons (chiffonade)

1. Trim the green beans and snap each bean in half.

2. Using the Sauté function, heat the olive oil in the pressure cooker. Add the onion and cook until softened, about 2 minutes. Add the garlic and cook until fragrant, about 1 minute. Turn off the Sauté function.

3. Add the green beans and tomatoes to the pressure cooker. Season lightly with salt and pepper and stir to combine. Cook on high pressure for 6 minutes.

4. Manually release the steam. If the sauce is too watery, use the Sauté function to bring it to a simmer. Cook, stirring occasionally, until almost all the liquid has evaporated, 3 to 5 minutes.

5. Add the basil and stir to combine. Taste, adding more salt and pepper if desired, before serving.

Braised Endive and Ham Gratin

Endives au jambon gratinées

Serves 4 as a light main course, or 6 as a side dish

Raw endives are common in winter salads, but before I lived in France, I had no idea people ate them cooked. This rustic dish is an ideal expression of butter-soft braised endives wrapped in ham and blanketed with béchamel sauce. Note that because the cooked endives produce a lot of liquid, which can turn the béchamel watery, they benefit from a gentle (but thorough) squeeze.

---

8 medium endives

2 tablespoons (30 grams) unsalted butter

3 tablespoons all-purpose flour

2 cups (500 ml) milk

Pinch of grated nutmeg, plus more as desired

Fine salt and freshly ground black pepper

8 thin slices ham, such as Virginia ham

¾ cup (120 grams) grated cheese, such as Gruyère, Comté, or Emmenthal

1. Place the steaming rack in the pressure cooker and add 1 cup (250 ml) water. Trim the base of each endive and pull off any discolored or wilted outer leaves. Arrange the endives on the rack in a single layer. Cook on high pressure for 7 minutes.

2. While the endives are cooking, in a medium saucepan, melt the butter over low heat. Add the flour and cook, stirring continuously, until the mixture smells slightly toasty, about 5 minutes. Pour in the milk and whisk until the mixture begins to thicken. Boil for 1 minute, whisking continuously. Remove béchamel sauce from heat and add the nutmeg. Season lightly with salt and pepper to taste.

3. When the endives have finished cooking, manually release the steam. Test an endive by piercing it with the tip of a paring knife. If there's any resistance, close and lock the lid of the pressure cooker and allow them to sit in the residual heat for 3 to 5 minutes before testing again. Transfer the endives to a plate.

4. Preheat the oven to 350°F (180°C).

5. When the endives are cool enough to handle, gently squeeze them to remove as much liquid as possible. Blot them dry with paper towels. Wrap each endive with a slice of ham and arrange them in a baking dish. Pour the béchamel sauce over the endives and sprinkle with the cheese. Bake for 20 to 25 minutes, or until sauce is bubbling. Switch the oven to broil and lightly brown the cheese, watching carefully to be sure it doesn't burn.

Winter Squash Gratin

Gratin de courge

Serves 4–6

In the winter months, Paris markets display enormous pumpkins that could double as Cinderella's carriage, sold by the slice, as thick or thin as you desire. Petite pumpkins are called potimarron, because their flavor is reminiscent of chestnuts, while butternut squash is known as le butternut. Any type of winter squash would work in this classic country recipe, which uses whipped egg whites to lighten the dense flesh of the gourd. Orange zest adds a note of sunshine, but sometimes I make this gratin without any spices, relying only on salt and pepper to season the warm, earthy squash. A dusting of grated cheese turns the top golden and crusty, but if you're not in the mood, feel free to leave that off, too.

---

2 pounds (1 kg) winter squash, such as pumpkin, butternut squash, or kabocha squash

4 tablespoons (60 grams) unsalted butter, melted, plus room-temperature butter for the pan

¼ cup (30 grams) bread crumbs

¾ cup (180 ml) milk

4 large eggs

½ teaspoon fine salt

½ teaspoon grated nutmeg (optional)

2 tablespoons orange zest (optional)

Freshly ground black pepper

1. Slice the squash into 1-inch-thick (2.5-cm) rings or wedges and seed them (if necessary).

2. Place the steaming rack in the pressure cooker and add 1 cup (250 ml) water. Arrange the squash on top. Cook on high pressure for 12 minutes.

3. While the squash is cooking, generously butter a shallow 6-cup baking dish and sprinkle it with the bread crumbs.

4. When the squash has finished cooking, manually release the steam. Transfer the squash to a plate to cool slightly.

5. Preheat the oven to 400°F (200°C).

6. When the squash is cool enough to handle, use a spoon to scrape the flesh from the tough skin; discard the skin. Transfer the flesh to a blender or food processor and puree. (Alternatively, put the squash flesh in a large bowl and puree it with an immersion blender.) Transfer the squash to a large bowl. Add the melted butter, milk, 2 eggs, the salt, nutmeg (if using), orange zest (if using), and pepper to

(continued)

¼ cup (30 grams)
grated Comté or Gruyère
cheese, or 1 tablespoon
(15 grams) unsalted
butter, cut into small
cubes

taste. Separate the remaining 2 eggs, adding the yolks to the squash mixture, and place the whites in a separate large bowl. Combine the egg yolks with the squash mixture.

7. Add a pinch of salt to the egg whites and beat with a whisk or handheld mixer until they hold stiff peaks. Fold the egg whites into the squash mixture, leaving some streaks of white.

8. Gently pour the squash mixture into the prepared baking dish. Sprinkle the grated cheese over the top or dot the surface with butter. Bake until the top is golden and the center appears set, 45 to 50 minutes.

Belgian Root Vegetable Mash

Stoemp

Serves 4–6

Pronounced "stoomp," this is comfort food at its finest, a cozy, stick-to-your-ribs mash of root vegetables that's delicious, cheap, easy to make—and even easier (and quicker) when cooked in the pressure cooker. Stoemp is traditionally eaten on cold winter nights, accompanied by fried sausages, boudin noir, or carbonade (page 96). Feel free to adapt stoemp to the seasons, replacing leeks and carrots with similar quantities of onions, turnips, cauliflower, broccoli, cabbage, chard, kale, Brussels sprouts, or any other winter green that strikes your fancy.

4 tablespoons (60 grams) unsalted butter

2 leeks, halved, rinsed well, and chopped

1 pound (500 grams) carrots, cut into rounds

2 pounds (1 kg) starchy potatoes like Russett, cut into 1-inch (2.5-cm) chunks

2 bay leaves

1 teaspoon dried thyme

2 teaspoons fine salt, plus more as desired

¼ teaspoon grated nutmeg, plus more as desired

Freshly ground black pepper

1. Using the Sauté function, melt the butter in the pressure cooker. Add the leeks and cook until softened, about 2 minutes. Turn off the Sauté function.

2. Add the carrots, potatoes, and 1 cup (250 ml) water to the pot. Stir in the bay leaves, thyme, and salt. Cook on high pressure for 5 minutes.

3. Manually release the steam. Remove the bay leaves from the vegetable mixture. Add the nutmeg and pepper to taste. Using a potato masher, crush the vegetables into a rustic puree. Taste and adjust the seasonings, adding more salt, pepper, and/or nutmeg as desired.

Braised Red Cabbage with Apples and Chestnuts

Chou rouge aux pommes et marrons

Serves 4

Sweet and tart, laced with apples and chestnuts, and boasting a beautiful, deep garnet color, this braised red cabbage is inspired by the cuisine of Alsace in eastern France, on the German border. In the past 150 years, Alsace has shifted several times between France and Germany, leaving the region with its own language, similar to Swiss-German, and a cuisine rich with German influence. This recipe is a wonderful accompaniment to roast pork, pork chops, or roast turkey. Who knows? It could even replace the cranberry sauce on your holiday table!

---

1 to 1½ pounds (500 to 750 grams) red cabbage (about ½ head)

1 tablespoon vegetable or olive oil

1 onion, sliced into half-moons

½ cup (125 ml) red wine

2 cooking apples, peeled, quartered, and cored

5 ounces (150 grams) vacuum-packed peeled chestnuts

2 tablespoons sugar, plus more as desired

1 bay leaf

Fine salt and freshly ground black pepper

1. Remove the core from the cabbage and cut it into three wedges. Slice each wedge into thin strips.

2. Using the Sauté function, heat the vegetable oil in the pressure cooker. Add the onion and cook until softened, about 2 minutes. Turn off the Sauté function.

3. Add the cabbage, wine, and ½ cup (125 ml) water to the pot. Stir in the apples, chestnuts, sugar, and bay leaf. Season lightly with salt and pepper. Cook on high pressure for 10 minutes.

4. Allow the steam to release naturally. Discard the bay leaf. Taste the cabbage and adjust the seasonings, adding more salt, pepper, and/or sugar as desired.

CHESTNUTS

Chestnuts, which grow widely in France, once sustained large swathes of the population. Highly nutritious, they can be roasted and eaten whole, ground into flour, or even preserved in sugar and enjoyed as a sweetmeat. These days, peeled chestnuts are most often sold in vacuum-sealed packets. A popular addition to turkey stuffing, in the States they're readily available during the holiday season, but can be difficult to locate the rest of the year. If you enjoy cooking with chestnuts—and they do add a lovely sweetness to braised Brussels sprouts, soups (like the butternut squash soup on page 26), or other desserts—you can often find them in Asian supermarkets, which stock them year-round.

Mushroom and Pea Risotto

Risotto aux champignons et petits pois

Serves 4

Risotto is, of course, Italian—but it is as popular in France as it is everywhere else, which is to say everyone loves it. Risotto is one of the truly magical pressure cooker recipes, perfect in only a few minutes, with almost zero stirring—it is finally a viable weeknight meal!

Almost any vegetable works well in risotto, but in this recipe, I've used mushrooms, which are coveted in France, especially wild varieties like cèpe (porcini), girolle (chanterelle), and oyster, which appear in the markets in the fall. But feel free to use cultivated brown button mushrooms if you wish—or substitute your favorite vegetables, anything from asparagus to artichoke to butternut squash.

---

3 tablespoons (45 grams) unsalted butter

½ cup (90 grams) finely chopped onion

1½ cups (330 grams) Arborio rice

½ cup (125 ml) dry white wine

3 to 3½ cups (750 to 875 ml) chicken stock

½ pound (250 grams) brown button mushrooms, sliced

Fine salt and freshly ground black pepper

1 cup (120 grams) frozen petite peas

1. Using the Sauté function, melt 1 tablespoon (15 grams) of the butter in the pressure cooker. Add the onion and cook until softened, about 2 minutes.

2. Add the rice to the pot and stir, coating the grains with the butter. Cook, stirring steadily, until the outer shell of the rice grains turns translucent, about 30 seconds. Add the wine and cook until almost all the liquid has evaporated. Turn off the Sauté function.

3. Add 3 cups of the stock and stir, scraping up any grains stuck to the bottom of the pot with a wooden spoon. Cook on high pressure for 4 minutes.

4. While the risotto is cooking, in a medium skillet, melt 1 tablespoon (15 grams) of the butter over medium heat until foamy. When the foam subsides, add the mushrooms to the pan and cook until tender, 3 to 4 minutes. Season lightly with salt and pepper and remove from the heat.

5. When the risotto has finished cooking, manually release the steam. It will look quite soupy. Using the Sauté function, bring the risotto to a rapid simmer and cook, stirring continuously, until the rice absorbs the liquid but still maintains its

¾ cup (75 grams) grated
  Parmesan cheese, plus
  more for serving
2 tablespoons chopped
  fresh herbs, such as mint,
  dill, fresh flat-leaf parsley,
  and/or chives (optional)

chewy bite, 1 to 3 minutes. Just before it attains your desired consistency, add the mushrooms and frozen peas, heating them through. If at any point the risotto becomes too dry, add a splash or two of stock to bring it back to the desired consistency. Turn off the Sauté function.

6. Stir in the remaining 1 tablespoon (15 grams) butter, the Parmesan, and the herbs (if using). Taste and adjust the seasonings, adding more salt and pepper as desired. Serve immediately, topped with additional Parmesan.

7

DESSERTS
Les Desserts

Strawberry-Rhubarb Compote

Compote à la rhubarbe et aux fraises

Serves 4–6

French people are fond of cooked fruit desserts, and this strawberry and rhubarb compote is a classic combination that's delicious with vanilla ice cream, lemon cake, or as a topping for your very own homemade yogurt (see page 171). In this recipe, the fruit is sweetened with maple syrup, which heightens the spring flavors, but the ratios are not an exact science, so feel free to reduce as you wish. Make sure to release the pressure from the cooker naturally, as the sticky froth of the syrup could clog the vent holes—to speed up the process, place a damp kitchen towel on top of the lid.

½ pound (250 grams) rhubarb, cut into 1-inch (2.5-cm) pieces

1 pound (500 grams) strawberries, hulled and halved

¼ cup (65 ml) maple syrup, plus more as desired

1 (2- to 3-inch / 2.5- to 7.5-cm) strip orange zest peeled with a vegetable peeler

1. In the pressure cooker, combine all the ingredients with ¼ cup (65 ml) water and stir to combine. Cook on high pressure for 2 minutes. Allow the pressure to release naturally.

2. Remove and discard the strip of orange zest. Carefully taste the compote (it is searing hot) and add more maple syrup, if desired.

3. Using the Sauté function, bring the compote to a brisk simmer and cook, stirring continuously, until reduced to the desired consistency. Allow the compote to cool completely before serving. Store in the refrigerator for up to 7 days.

Individual Chocolate Custards

Pots de crème au chocolat

Serves 6–8

Cold, silky, creamy, and chocolaty, these little desserts are best made in advance so they can chill completely in the fridge—which makes them perfect for dinner parties. The trick to perfect pressure cooker custard is to wrap each ramekin very tightly in foil, so that no unruly blasts of hot steam slip into the dish. If desired, serve each little pot dolloped with whipped cream and sprinkled with cocoa nibs, which add a lovely crunch.

1½ cups (375 ml) heavy cream
1½ cups (375 ml) whole milk
4 ounces (112 grams) bittersweet chocolate, finely chopped
5 egg yolks
1 large egg
¼ cup (50 grams) sugar
⅛ teaspoon fine salt
Whipped cream, for serving (optional)

1. In a small saucepan, bring the cream and milk to a boil. Remove from the heat, add the chocolate, and whisk until the chocolate has melted and the mixture is smooth.

2. In a large bowl, whisk together the egg yolks, egg, sugar, and salt. While whisking continuously, slowly pour the hot chocolate into the egg mixture. Strain through a fine-mesh sieve into a bowl or large measuring cup.

3. Divide the mixture among six 4-ounce (125-ml) oven-safe ramekins. Wrap each ramekin tightly with aluminum foil.

4. Place the steaming rack in the pressure cooker and add 1½ cups (375 ml) water. Place the ramekins on the rack, stacking them to fit, if necessary. Cook on high pressure for 8 minutes.

5. Allow the pressure to release naturally. Remove the custards from the pressure cooker and unwrap each one. The custards will be mostly set but still jiggle slightly in the center. Transfer the ramekins to a wire rack to cool completely. Cover and refrigerate for at least 3 hours before serving.

6. Serve topped with whipped cream, if desired.

Crème Brûlée

Crème brûlée

Serves 4–5

A bistro classic, this crowd-pleaser is simple and quick when made in the pressure cooker. I like a very thin layer of sugar crust, and so only use a small sprinkle on top—but if you prefer more crunch feel free to add a larger spoonful.

---

2 cups (500 ml) heavy cream
5 egg yolks
½ cup (100 grams) white granulated sugar, plus more for topping
1 teaspoon pure vanilla extract

1. In a saucepan, heat the cream until very hot but not boiling. Remove from the heat.

2. In a medium bowl, gently whisk together the egg yolks, sugar, and vanilla, trying not to create a lot of foam. Slowly whisk the hot cream into the egg mixture.

3. Divide the egg mixture among five 4-ounce (125-ml) oven-safe ramekins. Wrap each ramekin tightly with aluminum foil.

4. Place the steaming rack in the pressure cooker and add 1½ cups (375 ml) water. Place the ramekins on the rack, stacking them to fit, if necessary. Cook at high pressure for 8 minutes.

5. Allow the pressure to release naturally. Remove the custards from the pressure cooker and unwrap each one. The custards will be mostly set but still jiggle slightly in the center when shaken. Set the ramekins on a wire rack to cool.

6. To serve, sprinkle the top of each custard with a thin, even layer of sugar, ½ to 1 teaspoon each. Use a kitchen torch to melt and caramelize the sugar until dark golden brown. (Alternatively, preheat the broiler, place the ramekins on a baking sheet, and broil 2 to 3 inches/5 to 7.5 cm from the heat source until the sugar has melted and browned into a dark golden caramel shell.) Allow to cool for 5 minutes before serving.

Rice Pudding with Salted Butter Caramel

Riz au lait et sauce au caramel beurre salé

Serves 6–8

Sweet and milky, rice pudding is true French comfort food, the sort of thing Maman makes to fatten up her little ones, sometimes even serving it as a special cozy supper. Traditional riz au lait takes at least an hour to cook, the closely watched pot of milk and rice threatening to bubble over at any second—but the pressure cooker greatly speeds up and simplifies the process. In modern Paris bistros, riz au lait is often served with salted butter caramel sauce poured generously over the top.

⅔ cup (150 grams)
    Arborio rice
⅓ cup (80 grams) sugar
1¾ cups (400 ml)
    whole milk
Pinch of salt
1 vanilla bean
Salted Butter Caramel
    Sauce (page 158), for
    serving

1. In the pressure cooker, stir together the rice, sugar, milk, and salt. Split the vanilla bean in half lengthwise, scrape out the seeds, and add both the seeds and pod to the pot. Cook on low pressure for 14 minutes.

2. Make the Salted Butter Caramel Sauce (see page 158) while the rice is cooking.

3. When the rice has finished cooking, allow the pressure to release naturally. (Alternatively, allow the pressure to release naturally for 10 minutes, then manually release any remaining steam.) The rice pudding will appear quite soupy. Using the Sauté function, bring it to a boil and cook, stirring often, until the pudding thickens but is still slightly soupy, 2 to 3 minutes. Turn off the Sauté function. The rice pudding will continue to thicken as it stands.

4. Serve warm, in small dishes, drizzled generously with the caramel sauce.

(continued)

Salted Butter Caramel Sauce

Yields 1 cup

This decadent sauce is delicious drizzled over rice pudding, crêpes, apple slices . . . the possibilities are endless. A spoonful of corn syrup keeps the melting sugar from crystallizing, but if you're feeling confident, you can leave it out.

¾ cup (190 ml) heavy cream

1 cup (100 grams) white granulated sugar

1 tablespoon light corn syrup (optional)

3 tablespoons (45 grams) salted butter, cut into cubes

Pinch of fleur de sel (optional)

1. In a small saucepan, heat the cream over low heat until hot but not boiling.

2. In a large, deep saucepan, combine the sugar, corn syrup (if using), and ¼ cup (65 ml) water and heat over medium-high heat, swirling the pan occasionally—*but not stirring*—until sugar has melted and the syrup is a golden caramel color, 8 to 10 minutes. To avoid burning—which happens in a flash—remove the pan from the heat when the syrup is just on the verge of turning the desired dark caramel color. Continue swirling the pan as the color darkens. The syrup will retain enough heat to continue caramelizing.

3. Using a wire whisk, beat the hot cream into the syrup. Beat in the cubes of butter and the fleur de sel (if using) until melted and incorporated. Return the saucepan to medium heat and bring to a boil. Cook, stirring, for 2 to 3 minutes, until the sauce becomes smooth and glossy. At this stage the sauce is searingly hot so do not taste or touch it. Allow to cool completely before serving or storing. The sauce will keep in an airtight container in the refrigerator for a month.

Note: The sauce will thicken as it cools and will solidify in the fridge. Before serving, microwave it for about 15 seconds to warm it up; check the consistency, stir in a drizzle of cream or milk if needed, and microwave for another 10 seconds.

Rosemary Crème Caramel

Crème caramel au romarin

Serves 8

In French, crème caramel; in Spanish, flan—this slippery custard is cooked in a sophisticated, bittersweet sauce of caramelized sugar. I like perfuming the custard with rosemary, which adds a subtle botanical note. You can also use thyme or bay leaves—or feel free to omit.

---

3 (3- to 4-inch / 7.5- to
 10-cm) sprigs fresh
 rosemary
3 cups (750 ml) whole milk
1½ (300 grams) cups white
 granulated sugar
2 large eggs
3 egg yolks
1 teaspoon pure vanilla
 extract
Pinch of fine salt

1. Crush the rosemary sprigs with your hands to release their fragrance, then put them in a small saucepan. Add the milk and heat over medium heat until the milk turns foamy and is just about to boil. Turn off the heat, cover, and steep for about 15 minutes.

2. Meanwhile, place eight 4-ounce (125-ml) ramekins within easy reach. In a medium pot, combine 1 cup (200 grams) of the sugar and ¼ cup (60 ml) water and swirl to combine. Heat the mixture over medium-high heat, swirling the pan occasionally—*but do not stir* (this will cause crystals to form)—until the mixture comes to a rapid boil. Cook until the syrup becomes a golden caramel color, 6 to 8 minutes, then remove it from the heat and continue swirling the pan until it turns a deep walnut brown. (The syrup retains heat and will continue to caramelize off the heat.)

3. Moving swiftly, pour the caramel into the ramekins, dividing it evenly. Tilt each ramekin to coat the bottom evenly with the caramel.

4. In a large bowl, whisk together the eggs, egg yolks, vanilla, and remaining ½ cup (100 grams) sugar. Strain the milk, discarding the rosemary sprigs, and while whisking, slowly pour the hot milk into the egg mixture. Whisk until thoroughly combined.

(continued)

5. Strain the mixture through a fine-mesh sieve into another bowl or a large measuring cup. Divide the custard evenly among the ramekins. Wrap each ramekin tightly with aluminum foil.

6. Place the steaming rack in the pressure cooker and add 1½ cups (375 ml) water. Place the ramekins on the rack, stacking them to fit, if necessary. Cook on low pressure for 1 minute. (If you use ramekins of a different size or thickness, the time may vary.)

7. Allow the pressure to release naturally. Alternatively, allow the pressure to release naturally for 10 minutes, then manually release the steam. Remove the custards from the pressure cooker and unwrap each one. The custards will be mostly set but they should jiggle slightly in the center. Set them on a wire rack to cool slightly, then refrigerate them until completely chilled.

8. To serve, run a small, sharp knife around the outer edge of each custard. Invert onto individual serving plates, shaking the ramekin gently until the custard drops free and the caramel flows over the top in thin layers

THE BAIN-MARIE

A *bain-marie* is a water bath used to gently cook foods at a steady temperature. If you're cooking conventionally, you can create a *bain-marie* by filling a large roasting pan with boiling water, carefully setting your filled ramekins of custard within, and placing the whole setup in the oven. This can be messy as the hot liquid will threaten to slop from the pan every time you pull it from the oven.

Happily, the pressure cooker is an ideal *bain-marie*—hot and steamy, with an even temperature. All you need is a steaming rack and enough aluminum foil to tightly wrap your containers to protect the custard from condensation. With the pressure cooker, any worries about uneven temperatures and inaccurate cooking times are eliminated. You simply set the amount of time, and walk away.

Poached Pears with Chocolate Sauce

Poires Belle Hélène

Serves 4–6

Pears and chocolate combine in this classic dessert, which was named after an Offenbach operetta and is still served in the cafés that line the Grands Boulevards near Paris's Palais Garnier. Though this dessert seems complex, with the help of the pressure cooker, it becomes deceptively simple: The pears poach easily in the pressure cooker—and the microwave-friendly chocolate sauce can be made in just one minute. Accompany with a scoop of vanilla ice cream, if desired.

1½ cups (250 grams) sugar

1 (2- to 3-inch / 5- to 7.5-cm) strip lemon zest, peeled with a vegetable peeler

1 vanilla bean

4 to 6 firm pears, such as Bartlett

Chocolate Sauce (recipe follows), for serving

Vanilla ice cream, for serving (optional)

1. In the pressure cooker, combine the sugar, lemon zest, and 6 cups (1.5 L) water. Split the vanilla bean lengthwise, scrape out the seeds, and add the seeds and the pod to the pot. Mix well to combine.

2. Peel the pears, leaving the stem attached, and add them to the poaching liquid. Cook on high pressure for 7 minutes.

3. Allow the pressure to release naturally. (Alternatively, allow the pressure to naturally release for 10 minutes, then manually release the steam.) Remove the inner pot from the pressure cooker and allow the pears to cool in the poaching liquid.

4. Serve the pears in individual bowls, generously drizzled with chocolate sauce, with a scoop of vanilla ice cream, if desired.

(continued)

Chocolate Sauce

1 cup (185 grams) semi-
  sweet chocolate chips
¼ cup (60 ml) heavy cream
1 tablespoon dark rum, plus
  more as desired

1. In a medium microwave-safe bowl, combine the chocolate chips and cream. Microwave on high for 30 seconds. Stir and microwave for 30 seconds more, if necessary, to melt the chocolate. Whisk the sauce until glossy and smooth.

2. Whisk the rum into the sauce. Taste and add more rum as desired.

Note: The chocolate sauce will thicken as it cools; microwave in 15-second intervals, stirring after each, until it reaches the desired consistency. Drops of water (or condensation) can cause the sauce to seize up—to smooth it, add hot cream to the warmed sauce, 1 tablespoon at a time, and whisk until smooth.

Lemon–Goat Cheese Cheesecake

Fiadone

Serves 4–6

Located off the coast of southern France, the island of Corsica has a rugged cuisine rich in chestnut flour, sheep's-milk cheeses, and wild boar. Fiadone is a traditional dessert, a crustless cheesecake made with brocciu, a fresh sheep's-milk cheese found only on the island. A combination of ricotta and goat cheese is a worthy substitute, lending a distinct rustic note. Simple and gently sweet, fiadone is tender and moist, and perfumed with lemon zest, and either Grand Marnier or—traditionally—brandy. Enjoy it as the Corsicans do: for breakfast.

Butter, for greasing the pan

7 ounces (200 grams) whole-milk ricotta cheese

7 ounces (200 grams) goat cheese, at room temperature

3 large eggs

1/3 cup plus 1 tablespoon (80 grams) sugar

Zest of 1 lemon

2 teaspoons liqueur, such as Grand Marnier, or brandy

SPECIAL EQUIPMENT

7-inch springform pan

1. Generously butter the springform pan. Place the steaming rack in the pressure cooker and add 1½ cups (375 ml) water.

2. In a large bowl using a handheld mixer, beat together the ricotta and goat cheese.

3. In a separate bowl using the mixer, beat together the eggs and sugar—but don't whip air into the mixture, as you don't want the cheesecake to rise. Add the ricotta mixture, lemon zest, and liqueur and beat until thoroughly combined.

4. Pour the batter into the prepared pan. Cover tightly with aluminum foil. Place the pan on the steaming rack in the pressure cooker. If you do not have a steaming rack, use a long sheet of folded aluminum foil to create a sling to lift the springform pan out of the inner pot. Cook on high pressure for 13 minutes.

5. Allow the pressure to release naturally. (Alternatively, allow the steam to release naturally for 10 minutes, then manually release the remaining pressure.) Unwrap the cake and insert a small sharp knife into the center; if it comes out clean, the cake is done. If not, cover the pan with the foil, return it to the pressure cooker, close and lock the lid, and allow to sit in the residual heat for 5 to 10 minutes before testing again.

(continued)

6. Preheat the broiler. Line a baking sheet with foil.

7. Remove the cake from the pressure cooker and place it on a foil-lined baking sheet. Uncover the cake and blot any moisture on the surface with a paper towel. Broil until the top of the cake is golden brown, watching closely so it does not burn. Allow to cool, then refrigerate until chilled. Remove the outer ring of the pan, and serve.

David Lebovitz's Foolproof Chocolate Cake

Gâteau au chocolat infaillible de David Lebovitz

Serves 6–8

This recipe was inspired by David Lebovitz's Orbit Cake, a creation so foolproof he nicknamed it "choco-late idiot cake"—and the pressure cooker makes an easy recipe even easier. The cake is very rich, so serve it in thin slices, with a dollop of whipped cream to cut the intense chocolatiness.

¾ cup (1½ sticks / 170 grams) unsalted butter, plus more for greasing the pan

Unsweetened cocoa powder, for dusting the pan

8 ounces (225 grams) dark chocolate

4 large eggs

¾ cup (150 grams) sugar

Whipped cream, for serving

SPECIAL EQUIPMENT
7-inch springform pan

1. Generously butter the springform pan and dust the bottom and sides with cocoa powder, tapping out any excess. Place the steaming rack in the pressure cooker and add 1½ cups (375 ml) water.

2. In the top of a double boiler or a heatproof bowl set over a saucepan of simmering water (be sure the bottom of the bowl doesn't touch the water), melt the chocolate and butter, stirring occasionally, until smooth and glossy. Remove from the heat. (Alternatively, combine the chocolate and butter in a microwave-safe bowl and microwave in 30-second increments, stirring after each, until smooth and glossy.)

3. In a large bowl, whisk together the eggs and sugar until combined. Allow the chocolate to cool slightly and then pour it into the egg and sugar mixture, whisk-ing until smooth. Pour the batter into the prepared pan. Cover the pan tightly with aluminum foil. Place the pan on the steaming rack in the pressure cooker. Cook on high pressure for 22 minutes.

4. Allow the pressure to release naturally. (Alternatively, allow the steam to release naturally for 10 minutes, then manually release the remaining pressure.) Remove the cake from the pressure cooker and remove the foil. The cake should be just set in the center, and a fingertip touched to the surface should come away almost clean. Set the cake on a wire rack to cool completely.

5. Remove the outer ring of the pan. Serve in very thin slices at room temperature, accompanied with whipped cream, as desired.

"Baked" Apples

Pommes "au four"

Serves 4

This old-fashioned dessert rarely finds its way onto French restaurant menus, perhaps because of its simple, homey appearance. Whole apples are filled with walnuts, raisins, and sugar and softened in the pressure cooker in only a few minutes. Note that a pinch of cinnamon is optional—the strong spice is divisive in France, with vanilla more commonly used for apple desserts. Soft and sweet, these wholesome apples are delicious accompanied with heavy cream, crème fraîche, or vanilla ice cream—or a drizzle of Salted Butter Caramel Sauce (see page 158).

¼ cup (30 grams) finely chopped walnuts

¼ cup (40 grams) lightly packed light brown sugar

1 teaspoon pure vanilla extract

2 tablespoons raisins or currants

1 teaspoon ground cinnamon (optional)

4 firm medium apples of equal size, such as Honeycrisp, Granny Smith, or Jonagold

1 tablespoon (15 grams) unsalted butter

Vanilla ice cream or heavy cream, for serving

SPECIAL EQUIPMENT

8-inch round soufflé dish

1. In a small bowl, combine the walnuts, brown sugar, vanilla, raisins, and cinnamon (if using).

2. Using a paring knife, cut out the stem from each apple, creating a small hole. Then use a spoon to dig out the core and seeds.

3. Arrange the apples in the dish and spoon the sugar mixture into their centers. Divide the butter into 4 squares, placing one piece upon each apple.

4. Place the steaming rack in the pressure cooker and add 1 cup (250 ml) water. Place the dish with the apples on the rack. Cook on low pressure for 13 minutes.

5. Allow the pressure to release naturally. (Alternatively, allow the steam to release naturally for 10 minutes, then manually release the remaining pressure.) Slide a small sharp knife through the side of each apple. If there is any resistance, return them to the pressure cooker, close and lock the lid, and allow them to sit in the residual heat for 5 to 10 minutes before testing again.

6. Remove the dish of apples from the pressure cooker. Serve warm or at room temperature, with a scoop of vanilla ice cream or a drizzle of heavy cream.

Plain Yogurt

Yaourt nature

Serves 8–10

The yogurt aisle in a French supermarket can stretch eight rows deep, and though the flavors are numerous and unique, plain remains the most popular. Yogurt is an important part of French cuisine, often enjoyed at the end of a simple lunch or dinner as dessert. Making yogurt in the multifunctional pressure cooker is unbelievably easy, and the result is so creamy and delicious, you may never buy yogurt at the store again.

2 quarts (2 L) whole milk

3 tablespoons plain yogurt

SPECIAL EQUIPMENT
Instant read thermometer

1. Pour the milk into the pressure cooker. Cover and bring the milk to a boil using the Yogurt function, adjusting until the screen reads "Boil." Allow the boiled milk to stand for 5 minutes before turning off the pressure cooker.

2. Remove the inner pot from the pressure cooker, place it on a wire rack, and allow the milk to cool to 115°F, stirring occasionally and testing it with an instant-read thermometer, about 30 minutes.

3. In a medium bowl, combine the yogurt with ⅔ cup (160 ml) of the warmed milk. Pour this mixture back into the pot of warmed milk and return the pot to the pressure cooker. Cover and use the Yogurt function to incubate the mixture for 8 hours.

4. When the incubation time has finished, turn off the pressure cooker. Transfer the yogurt to clean jars or other airtight containers, cover, and refrigerate overnight to thicken. If desired, strain the yogurt through cheesecloth for a thicker texture. Yogurt will keep for about 2 weeks in the refrigerator.

Index